D1580613

Contract Law

LIVERPOOL JMU LIBRARY

3 1111 01490 3213

YOU'VE GOT IT
CRACKED

Nutcases – your essential revision and starter guides

- Provides you with in-depth case analysis of the facts, principles and decision of the most important cases in an area of law

- Incorporates colour to help distinguish cases and legislation and aid ease of use

- Presents the text in bite-size chunks and includes bullets where appropriate to aid navigation, assimilation and retention of information

- Breaks the subject down into key topics to enable you to easily identify and concentrate on particular topics

- Opens each chapter with a short introduction to outline the key concepts covered and condense complex and important information

- Includes boxed "think points" at the end of each chapter providing further case analysis

- Fully indexed by individual cases and topics

Available from all good booksellers

SWEET & MAXWELL

THOMSON REUTERS

NUT**SHELLS**

Contract Law

TENTH EDITION

by
ROBERT DUXBURY, LL.B.
Barrister,
Former Principal Lecturer in Law,
Nottingham Law School,
Nottingham Trent University

SWEET & MAXWELL

 THOMSON REUTERS

Published in 2015 by Thomson Reuters (Professional) UK Limited
trading as Sweet & Maxwell, Friars House, 160 Blackfriars Road, London, SE1 8EZ
(Registered in England & Wales, Company No 1679046.
Registered Office and address for service:
2nd Floor, 1 Mark Square, Leonard Street, London, EC2A 4EG

Typeset by YHT Ltd

Printed in Great Britain by
CPI Group (UK) Ltd, Croydon, CR0 4YY

No natural forests were destroyed to make this product;
only farmed timber was used and re-planted

A CIP catalogue record for this book is available from the British Library.

ISBN: 978-0-414-03583-6

Thomson Reuters and the Thomson Reuters logo are trademarks of Thomson Reuters.
Sweet & Maxwell ® is a registered trademark of Thomson Reuters (Professional) UK
Limited.

Crown copyright material is reproduced with the permission of the Controller
of HMSO and the Queen's Printer for Scotland.

All rights reserved. No part of this publication may be reproduced or transmitted in any
form or by any means, or stored in any retrieval system of any nature without prior written
permission, except for permitted fair dealing under the Copyright, Designs and Patents Act
1988, or in accordance with the terms of a licence issued by the Copyright Licensing Agency
in respect of photocopying and/or reprographic reproduction. Application for permission
for other use of copyright material including permission to reproduce extracts in other
published works shall be made to the publishers. Full acknowledgement of author,
publisher and source must be given.

© 2015 Thomson Reuters (Professional) UK Limited

Contents

Using this book

CHAPTER INTRODUCTIONS open every chapter, providing an overview of the topic to be discussed.

The Basis of Interv

INTRODUCTION

The process of judicial review involve
made by bodies exercising public
ⁿ legality of these decisions

...re in au

...rendant is involved in a
to win.

CHECKPOINT

Approach adopted to incidents b
sporting events:
- In *Condon v Basi* (CA, 1985), a "ⁿ
  local amateur football match w
- In *Watson v British Boxing Boc*
  out that where the plaintiff cⁿ
  boxing ring he does not con
  safety arrangements by 'ⁿ

CHECKPOINTS highlight key concepts and define complex terms, boxed for easy identification and revision.

KEY CASES present the facts and judgments in the most influential case-law, boxed for easy identification and revision.

... comⁿ
...u secondly, since the
plaintiff cannot be said to cons
time (*Baker v T. E. Hopkins & Soⁿ*

KEY CASE

DANGER INVITES RESCUE; RESCUERS
RESCUE IS TO SAVE LIFE OR LIMB.
Chadwick v British Transport Com
assisted at the scene of a train cra
as a result of what he saw was hⁿ
was in no personal danger (for 'ⁿ
generally see Ch.2).

LEGISLATION HIGHLIGHTERS provide
extracts of the significant legislation,
boxed for easy identification and revision.

LEGISLATION HIGHLIGHTER

Section 149 of the Road Traffic Act (19
the driver's liability to his passenger
means that the *volenti* defence is now
road traffic accidents.

4. Rescuers
If the defendant's negligence endang
rescue attempt is reasonably fores
vnes v Harwood (CA, 1935))
is actually the

COLOUR CODING throughout to
help distinguish cases and legislation
from the narrative.

equent case law has decided
(a) Jews are an ethnic group (*Seide v*
(b) Gypsies are an ethnic group (*CRE v*
(c) Rastafarians are not an ethnic group
   ment [1993] I.R.L.R. 284)
(d) Jehovah's Witnesses are not an ethnic
   Norwich City College case 1502237/97
(e) RRA covers the Welsh (*Gwynedd CC v*
(f) Both the Scots and the English are co
   "national origins" but not by "ethn
   Board v Power [1997], *Boyce v Brit*

should be noted that Sikh
also

DIAGRAMS AND FLOWCHARTS condense and visually represent detailed information.

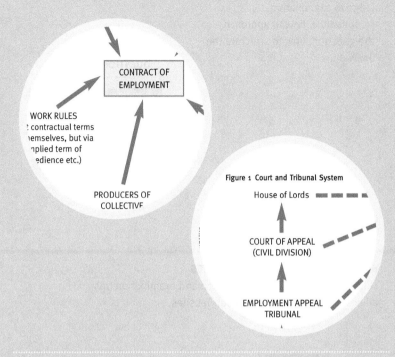

CONTRACT OF
EMPLOYMENT

WORK RULES
contractual terms
emselves, but via
nplied term of
edience etc.)

PRODUCERS OF
COLLECTIVE

Figure 1 Court and Tribunal System

House of Lords

COURT OF APPEAL
(CIVIL DIVISION)

EMPLOYMENT APPEAL
TRIBUNAL

END OF CHAPTER REVISION
CHECKLISTS identify the key take-aways from the chapter.

..us held th..
 liable because the pre₅
alleged negligence that, as the
criminal offence.

REVISION CHECKLIST

You should now understand:

☐ **The conditions within which the**
and the overlap between the def

☐ *Volenti* **is a complete defence ar**
because it is more flexible;

**END OF CHAPTER QUESTION AND
ANSWER SECTION** is a chance to practice what
you have learnt, with advice on relating knowledge to examination
performance, how to approach
the question, how to structure the
answer.

QUESTION AND ANSWE.

QUESTION

To what extent is a defendant in a t
was engaged in an illegal activity a

APPROACH TO THE ANSWER

Outline the effect of *ex tu*
action can be founds

HANDY HINTS AND USEFUL WEBSITES
close the book, with helpful revision and examination tips and
advice, along with a list of useful websites.

HANDY HINTS

Examination questions in employme.
either essay questions or problem que:
format and in what is required of the ex
of question in turn.
Students usually prefer one type
normally opting for the problem ques
examinations are usually set in a wa
least one of each style of questior
Very few, if any, questions
ows about a topic, and it
make a p

USEFUL WEBSITES

Official Information
www.parliament.uk—very user-friendly.
www.direct.gov.uk—portal for governm
www.opsi.gov.uk—Office of Public Sect
and statutory instruments available
www.dca.gov.uk—Department for Con
www.dca.gov.uk/peoples-rights/hur
Unit at the Department for Con
www.homeoffice.gov.uk/police
the **Police and Criminal**

Table of Cases

Table of Statutes

Introduction

THE LAW OF CONTRACT

The law of contract is a subject of great practical significance. In order to live, we enter into contracts every day. We may take a train or bus to work, buy food and drink or other goods, go to the cinema or a restaurant. We may also be subject to longer-term dealings, such as a contract of employment, a lease or a mortgage, or a finance agreement for the purchase of a car or other consumer goods. All of these transactions are governed by the law of contract. Contract is therefore not merely essential for the smooth functioning of business and commerce, but it underpins society itself.

The "law of contract" may be described as a body of rules relating to the enforceability of agreements between members of society, and the remedies available for the failure to fulfil those agreements. Most of the time contracts work perfectly well. It is only really *where things go wrong* that the law of contract comes into play. For example, the terms of the contract may be too vague to be enforceable, or there may have been a serious breach of the contract, or one party may have misled the other with a false statement, or the parties may be under a fundamental mistake as to what the contract is about, and so on. Contract law may provide the solution to such problems by, for example, declaring the contract to be null and void or giving a remedy, such as a claim for damages, to the injured party.

We now need to ask the question, what is the definition of a contract?

CHECKPOINT

A contract may be defined as an agreement between two or more parties that is binding in law. This means that the agreement generates rights and obligations that may be enforced in the courts. The normal method of enforcement is an action for damages for breach of contract, although in some cases the court may compel performance by the party in default.

THE CLASSICAL THEORY OF "FREEDOM OF CONTRACT"

Many of the principles of English contract law were developed in the eighteenth and nineteenth centuries under the classical doctrine of "freedom of contract". By this theory the parties are free to enter into whatever transactions they wish with a minimum of interference by the courts or government. However, once they have entered the agreement, they are strictly bound even if the contract turns out to be a "bad bargain" for them. The law will only intervene in cases of fraud, illegality or other legal wrong. The theory breaks down in the face of inequality of bargaining power, and in the twentieth century the courts (through judicial decisions) and Parliament (through legislation) have intervened to protect weaker parties, such as consumers, tenants and employees.

CONTEMPORARY INFLUENCES ON CONTRACT LAW

There are influences on English contract law that derive from international sources. Thus, European Community directives have been transposed into domestic contract law to regulate, for example, unfair terms in consumer contracts and distance selling contracts. Another potential influence on domestic contract law is the European Convention on Human Rights. Under the Human Rights Act 1998, legislation can be declared incompatible with Convention rights by the courts. This possibility was confirmed by *Wilson v Secretary of State for Trade and Industry*, HL, 2004, although in the case itself the particular provision in the Consumer Credit Act 1974 was ultimately found not to be incompatible.

In addition to the above measures, there have been moves to harmonise contract law in member States of the European Union. A set of "Principles of European Contract Law" has been published—the principles do not have the force of law, but they point the way towards possible future harmonisation.

CLASSIFICATION OF CONTRACTS

The traditional classification of contracts is divided into "deeds" and "simple contracts".

Deeds
The deed is of ancient origin and derives its validity from the form in which it is made. It must be in writing and must be signed, witnessed and delivered.

Promises made by deed do not need to be supported by consideration (see Chapter 4) in order to be enforceable.

Simple Contracts

All other contracts may be classified as simple contracts, whether they are made in writing, orally or by conduct. The law of simple contracts is the subject matter of this book.

Another way of classifying contracts is according to whether they are "bilateral" or "unilateral".

Bilateral Contracts

Here a promise by one party is exchanged for a promise by the other. The exchange of the promises is enough to render them both enforceable; thus, in a contract for the sale of goods, the buyer promises to pay the price and the seller promises to deliver the goods.

Unilateral Contracts

Here one party promises to do something in return for an *act* of the other party, as opposed to a promise, e.g. where A promises a reward to anyone who will find his lost wallet. The essence of the unilateral contract is that only one party, A, is bound to do anything. No one is bound to search for the lost wallet, but if B, having seen the offer, recovers the wallet and returns it, he is entitled to the reward. (Unilateral contracts are discussed in Chapter 2.)

. . . .

ELEMENTS OF THE LAW OF CONTRACT

There are three basic elements in the formation of a valid simple contract. First, the parties must have reached agreement (usually tested by offer and acceptance); secondly, they must intend to be legally bound; and thirdly, both parties must have provided valuable consideration. These matters are dealt with in Chapters 2–4.

In addition, the parties must have the legal capacity to contract, and, in some cases, there must be compliance with certain formalities (see Chapter 5).

A contract consists of various terms, both express and implied. A term may be inserted into the contract to exclude or restrict one party's liability (see Chapters 6 and 7).

A contract may be invalidated by a mistake, or by illegality (see Chapters 9 and 11), and where the contract has been induced by misrepresentation, duress or undue influence, the innocent party may have the right to set it aside (see Chapters 8 and 10).

At common law, third parties had no rights under a contract but this rule is subject to many exceptions and has been substantially modified by legislation (see Chapter 12). The discharge of contracts and the remedies available are dealt with in Chapters 13 and 14.

Offer and Acceptance

2

INTRODUCTION

The rules of offer and acceptance are concerned with whether the parties have reached agreement.

The main elements are:

(a) What constitutes in law an offer.

(b) The distinction between an offer and an invitation to treat.

(c) What constitutes the acceptance of an offer.

(d) The circumstances in which an offer may be terminated.

If a contract is a legally binding agreement, the first question to consider is the method by which the courts ascertain whether a contract has been formed. Formerly, the courts were concerned with whether there had been a meeting of the minds of the two parties, or *consensus ad idem*. The approach is now objective, i.e. whether a reasonable observer would assume an agreement to have been concluded on certain terms. The conventional formula for this is to consider whether one party (the offeror) has made an offer which has been accepted by the other (the offeree) so as to conclude a contract. The objective approach is illustrated by *Moran v University College Salford (No.2)*, CA, 1996, where a university applicant was made an unconditional offer of a place in error. It was held that the claimant's acceptance concluded a binding contract despite the error, of which the claimant was unaware. Offer and acceptance will now be considered in turn.

OFFER

> **CHECKPOINT**
>
> An offer may be defined as a statement of willingness to contract on specified terms made with the intention that, if accepted, there will arise a binding contract. An offer may be express or implied from conduct. It may be addressed to one particular person, a group of persons, or the world at large, as in an offer of a reward.

The leading "reward" case is discussed below.

KEY CASE

CARLILL V CARBOLIC SMOKE BALL CO., CA, 1893

The defendants advertised that they would pay £100 to anyone who contracted influenza after using their product for a specified period. As proof of their sincerity, the defendants stated that they had deposited £100 in a bank. The claimant contracted influenza after purchasing and using one as directed, and claimed the reward. The defendants argued, inter alia, that it was impossible to contract with the whole world.

Held: This argument was rejected by the court which found that the advertisement constituted an offer to the world at large, accepted by the claimant, who was entitled to the £100.

Comment

The contract in this case is a classic example of a unilateral contract. It should be noted that in court further defences were raised, including (i) that there was no contract because there had been no communication of acceptance; and (ii) that the advertisement was "mere puff" and not intended to be legally binding. Point (i) is discussed later in this chapter; and point (ii) in Chapter 3.

The above decision was relied upon by the Court of Appeal in *Bowerman v Association of British Travel Agents Ltd*, CA, 1995. It was held that the association had made a unilateral offer to prospective customers to provide protection in the event of the financial failure of one of its members. The offer was accepted by booking a holiday with an association member.

A genuine offer must be distinguished from an "invitation to treat"; i.e. where a party is merely inviting offers, which they are then free to accept or reject. The distinction has arisen in the following areas.

Advertisements

Advertisements of goods for sale are normally construed as invitations to treat.

KEY CASE

PARTRIDGE V CRITTENDEN, 1968

The appellant, who placed an advertisement in a periodical which said "Bramblefinches, 25 shillings each" was charged with the statutory offence of "offering for sale" a wild bird. He was convicted and he appealed.

> **Held:** His conviction would be quashed because the advertisement was not an offer but an invitation to treat.
>
> **Comment**
> It must be stressed that advertisements may be construed as offers if they are of the unilateral type, such as offers for rewards; see the *Carlill* case above.

In addition to advertisements, all circulars, catalogues and price lists distributed by traders will normally be regarded as invitations to treat; *Grainger and Sons v Gough*, HL, 1896. The reason for this approach is the so-called "quantity argument" whereby, if the advertisement amounted to an offer, the advertiser would be liable to all persons who purported to accept the offer, even if the advertiser had insufficient stocks to meet the demand.

Invitations to Tender
The courts have held that an invitation to tender will not normally amount to an offer to contract with the party submitting the most favourable tender; *Spencer v Harding*, 1870. However, it is now clear that an invitation to tender may amount to an offer of the unilateral type if that is what was clearly intended. In *Harvela Investments Ltd v Royal Trust Co of Canada (CI) Ltd*, HL, 1985, the first defendants invited the claimants and the second defendants to make sealed competitive bids for a parcel of shares, stating, "we bind ourselves to accept (the highest) offer". The claimants bid $2,175,000 and the second defendants bid $2,100,000 or $101,000 "in excess of any other offer". The first defendants believed that they were bound to accept the bid of the second defendants, as being the higher bid. The House of Lords held that the invitation to tender amounted to an offer to sell to the highest bidder; however, the "referential" bid of the type adopted by the second defendants was not permissible in a transaction of this kind and therefore the first defendants were bound to accept the claimants' bid.

A further case on tenders is *Blackpool & Fylde Aero Club Ltd v Blackpool Borough Council*, CA, 1990. Here the defendants invited tenders for an airport concession, laying down a clear procedure for the submission of bids. Due to an administrative error on the part of the defendants, the claimant's bid, which had been properly submitted, was not considered. The Court of Appeal held that the defendants were contractually bound to consider the claimant's tender.

Auction Sales
In an auction, the auctioneer's request for bids is an invitation to treat and each bid is an offer; *Payne v Cave*, 1789. This is given statutory force by

s.57(2) of the Sale of Goods Act 1979 which states "a sale by auction is complete when the auctioneer announces its completion by the fall of the hammer, or in other customary manner. Until such announcement is made, any bidder may retract his bid". Similarly, an advertisement that an auction will be held is not an offer; *Harris v Nickerson*, 1873. However, in *Warlow v Harrison*, 1859 it was stated, obiter, that an advertisement to hold an auction "without reserve" would amount to an offer to sell to the highest bidder, accepted by the submission of the highest bid. This approach was followed by the Court of Appeal in *Barry v Heathcote Ball & Co (Commercial Auctions)*, CA, 2000, where it was held that, in a sale without reserve, there was a collateral contract (see Chapter 6) between the auctioneer and the highest bidder. There was consideration both in the form of detriment to the bidder, since his bid could be accepted, and benefit to the auctioneer, as the bidding was driven up. It follows that, in such a sale, if the auctioneer refuses to sell to the highest bidder, they will be in breach of contract.

Display of Goods

KEY CASE

FISHER V BELL, 1960
The defendant shopkeeper displayed a flick knife in his shop window with the price attached. He was charged with the statutory offence of offering for sale such a knife. He was convicted and he appealed.

Held: The display of goods in such circumstances is no more than an invitation to treat—the defendant had not offered the goods for sale and was therefore acquitted.

Comment
It should be noted that the same principle had been applied earlier by the Court of Appeal to the display of goods in self-service stores; *Pharmaceutical Society of Great Britain v Boots Cash Chemists (Southern) Ltd*, CA, 1953. The main practical consequences of this are that under the law of contract, shops are not bound to sell goods at the price indicated; and a customer cannot demand to buy a particular item on display.

Sales of Land

In transactions involving land, it is sometimes more difficult to distinguish an offer from what are merely steps in negotiation. Thus, in one case, a council, in pursuance of a policy of selling council houses, wrote to a tenant, stating that they "may be prepared to sell the house" to him at a stated price. The tenant submitted a formal application but the transaction was broken off at that point by a change in the council's policy. The House of Lords held that there was no contract; the tenant's application was an offer rather than an acceptance; *Gibson v Manchester CC*, HL, 1979.

A statement of the minimum price at which a party may be willing to sell will not amount to an offer. In *Harvey v Facey*, PC, 1893, the claimants cabled the defendants, "Will you sell us Bumper Hall Pen? Telegraph lowest cash price." The defendants replied, "Lowest cash price for Bumper Hall Pen, $900." The claimants then cabled the defendants, "We agree to buy Bumper Hall Pen for the $900 asked by you." It was held that there was not a contract as the second telegram did not constitute an offer.

. . . .

ACCEPTANCE

CHECKPOINT

Acceptance may be defined as an unconditional assent, communicated by the offeree to the offeror, to all terms of the offer, made with the intention of accepting. Whether an acceptance has in fact occurred is ascertained objectively from the behaviour of the parties, including any correspondence that has passed between them.

It should be noted here that a contract will not be binding unless the parties have expressed themselves with reasonable certainty. The subject of certainty of terms is dealt with in Chapter 6. In relation to acceptance, the courts have developed the following rules.

Acceptance Must be Unconditional

The offeree must accept the exact terms proposed by the offeror unconditionally, i.e. without introducing any new terms which the offeror has not had the opportunity to consider. The introduction of new terms is referred to as a "counter-offer" and its effect in law is to bring to an end the original offer. For example, in *Hyde v Wrench*, 1840, the defendant offered to sell a farm to the claimant for £1,000. In reply, the claimant offered £950. This was rejected by the defendant. Later, the claimant purported to accept the original offer of £1,000. It was held there was no contract; the counter-offer of £950 had impliedly rejected the original offer which was no longer capable of acceptance.

Figure 1: Counter-offer

No contract: original offer destroyed

A counter-offer should be distinguished from a mere request for information as in *Stevenson v McLean*, 1880 where, in response to an offer to sell goods at a stated price made by the defendants, the claimants replied inquiring whether delivery could be made over two months. No reply to this inquiry was received but the claimants accepted the offer. It was held that there was a binding contract: the claimant's reply was a request for information and not a counter-offer.

Battle of the Forms

Figure 2: Battle of the Forms

Binding contract: counter-offer
accepted by conduct

The counter-offer analysis has been applied to the so-called "battle of the forms" where one party, A, makes an offer on a document containing his standard terms of business and the other party, B, "accepts" on a document containing his (conflicting) standard terms. At this stage, there is clearly no contract, although the courts have held that if B's communication is acted on by A, e.g. by delivery of goods, a contract may come into being on B's terms on the basis that his counter-offer has been accepted by conduct; *British*

Road Services v Arthur Crutchley Ltd, CA, 1968. This "traditional" approach was adopted by the Court of Appeal in *Butler Machine Tool Ltd v Ex-Cell-O Corp*, CA, 1979 and in *Tekdata Interconnections Ltd v Amphenol Ltd*, CA, 2009.

Acceptance of Tenders

We have seen that an invitation to tender is usually, but not invariably, an invitation to treat. Where this is the case, the tender constitutes an offer, however, the "acceptance" of a tender does not always result in a contract. It seems that there are three possibilities:

(1) If a party invites tenders for the supply of a specific quantity of goods on a specific date, then acceptance of the tender results in a binding contract.

(2) If tenders are invited for the supply of a specific quantity of goods over a period of time then, again, acceptance will conclude a contract.

(3) If the invitation to tender does not specify the quantity of goods, but requires the supply of goods in such quantity as may be ordered from time to time, or "as and when required", then "acceptance" of the tender does not at that stage conclude a contract. Any tender submitted is a "standing offer" which is only accepted in the legal sense when an order is placed for a quantity of goods and there will result a binding contract confined to that quantity; *Percival Ltd v LCC Asylums Committee*, 1918. The standing offer may be revoked at any time although the tenderer will be bound by orders already made; *G.N.R. v Witham*, 1873.

Acceptance Must be Communicated

As a general rule, acceptance will not be effective unless communicated to the offeror by the offeree or by someone with his or her authority. An uncommunicated mental assent will not suffice. In *The Leonidas D*, CA, 1985, Goff LJ said that it is "axiomatic that acceptance of an offer cannot be inferred from silence save in the most exceptional circumstances". The communication of acceptance must be actually received by the offeror, and, where the means of communication are instantaneous (oral, telephone, telex), the contract will come into being when and where acceptance is received; *Entores v Miles Far East Corp*, CA, 1955. A telex message sent during out-of-office hours would not be regarded as instantaneous and the time and place of the formation of the contract would be determined by the intentions of the parties, sound business practice and, possibly, on a judgment as to where the risk would lie; *Brinkibon v Stahag Stahl mbH*, HL, 1983.

The rule that acceptance must be communicated is subject to certain qualifications:

(1) Unilateral contracts. Here there is no requirement that acceptance

should be communicated and the performance of the stipulated act will constitute acceptance. Thus, in the *Carlill* case (see above) it was held that the contract was binding even though the claimant did not notify the defendants of her intention to accept.

(2) Need for communication dispensed with. It is possible, in a potentially bilateral contract, for the offeror, expressly or impliedly, to waive the need for communication of acceptance by the offeree, e.g. where goods are dispatched in response to an offer to buy. The acceptance in such a case takes place by conduct. It should, however, be clear that the particular conduct was performed by the offeree with the unequivocal intention of accepting the offer; *Taylor v Allon*, 1966, and *Day Morris Associates v Voyce*, CA, 2003. In *Anglia Television v Cayton*, 1989, it was said that it is a prerequisite of acceptance by conduct that there should be an unequivocal offer in a form capable of unequivocal acceptance. It is for the parties to agree a contract, not for the court to construe one on their behalf.

The above is subject to the reservation that it is not open to the offeror to impose a contract on the offeree against his wishes by deeming that his silence should amount to acceptance.

KEY CASE

FELTHOUSE V BINDLEY, 1862

The claimant wrote to his nephew offering to buy a horse and saying, "If I hear no more about him, I consider the horse mine at (a stated price)". The nephew did not reply but instructed an auctioneer to keep the horse out of a sale of the nephew's assets. The auctioneer, by mistake, included the horse in the sale and was sued by the claimant for conversion.

Held: The claimant had no title to sue since the nephew had not accepted his offer.

Comment
As it is clear that the nephew intended to accept the offer, it is at least arguable that his conduct in instructing the auctioneer not to sell the horse is consistent enough with such intention as to amount to acceptance. But in so far as *Felthouse v Bindley* embodies the principle that a contract cannot be imposed on an offeree, it is sound.

(3) Acceptance by post. This is dealt with below.

Method of Acceptance

If the offeror prescribes a particular method of communicating acceptance and makes it clear that no other method will suffice, then there may be no contract if a different method is used by the offeree; *Eliason v Henshaw*, 1819.

If, however, a method is prescribed without it being made clear that no other method will suffice, then it seems that an equally advantageous method would suffice. In *Tinn v Hoffman*, 1873 it was said that if the offeree was requested to reply "by return of post" then any method which would arrive no later than return of post would do. The Court of Appeal adopted the same approach in *Yates Building Co Ltd v Pulleyn Ltd*, CA, 1975. It is always open to the offeror, having prescribed a method of acceptance, to waive his right to insist on that method. Such waiver may be express or implied. In some cases the method of acceptance is prescribed by the offeree and inserted for his benefit, as in *Manchester Diocesan Council for Education v Commercial and General Investments Ltd*, 1969. Here the claimants invited tenders, requesting the tenderers to supply an address to which acceptances should be sent. The defendants' tender was accepted but the acceptance was sent to an address different to the one given by the tenderers. This was held to be a good acceptance; the claimants had introduced the prescribed method for their own protection and it could be waived by the claimants providing the defendants were not prejudiced.

Where the offer does not prescribe a method of acceptance, the appropriate method may be inferred from the form in which the offer is made; thus it was held in 1883 that if an offer is sent by telegram, a reply by post would be ineffective; *Quenerduaine v Cole*, 1883.

Acceptance by Post

A further exception to the rule that acceptance must be communicated is where acceptance is effected by post. The rule is that where acceptance by post has been requested, or where it is an appropriate and reasonable means of communication between the parties, then acceptance is complete immediately the letter of acceptance is posted, even if the letter is delayed, destroyed or lost in the post so that it never reaches the offeror; *Adams v Lindsell*, 1818.

HOUSEHOLD FIRE INSURANCE CO V GRANT, CA, 1879

The acceptance of G's offer to buy shares in the claimant company was posted to him but he never received it. When the company was wound up, G refused to pay for the shares.

Held: The contract was concluded on posting and G had therefore become a shareholder.

Comment

It seems that the rule applies to communications of acceptance by cable, including inland telemessages, but not to instantaneous modes such as telephone, telex, or fax machines.

The "postal rule" is essentially a rule of convenience and is usually justified on the grounds that if the offeror chooses the post as a means of effecting a contract, they must accept the inherent risks. The postal rule will not apply in the situations given below where the court may conclude that the contract comes into being when the letter of acceptance arrives. Where the offer has lapsed by the time the letter of acceptance arrives, then if the postal rule does not apply, there may be no contract at all.

The postal rule will not apply:

(1) where the letter of acceptance has not been properly posted, as in *Re London and Northern Bank*, 1900, where the letter of acceptance was handed to a postman only authorised to deliver;

(2) where the letter is not properly addressed. There is no direct authority on this point but the analogous case of *Getreideimport GmbH v Contimar*, 1953 would support this view. G. H. Treitel, *Law of Contract*, has suggested that an inflexible rule on this point might in some cases prejudice the offeror and the better rule is that a misdirected acceptance should take effect, if at all, at the time least favourable to the party responsible for misdirection. This analysis was accepted, obiter, by Toulson J in *Korbetis v Transgrain Shipping BV*, 2005;

(3) where the express terms of the offer exclude the postal rule, i.e. if the offer specifies that the acceptance must reach the offeror. In *Holwell Securities v Hughes*, CA, 1974, the postal rule was held not to apply where the offer was to be accepted by "notice in writing". Actual communication was required;

(4) where it is unreasonable to use the post; e.g. to reply by second class post to a verbal offer, or to accept by post on the eve of a postal strike. Further, it was said in Holwell's case (above) that the postal rule would

not be applied where it would produce a "manifest inconvenience or absurdity".

Although there is no English authority on the point, it does not seem possible, where the postal rule applies, for the offeree, having posted his acceptance, then to revoke it by some quicker means of communication, such as by telephone. The Scottish case of *Dunmore v Alexander*, 1830, which appears to permit such a revocation, is unreliable as the majority of the court seem to have decided the case on the basis that there had been the revocation of an offer.

Email

Communications by email bear some resemblance to postal communications in that the message is sent via an online server (akin to an electronic sorting office) and may not be immediately received. If the postal rule applied, the contract would come into being at the moment the offeree's mouse clicked on the "send" button. However, since the sender will generally know if his message has not been sent, it seems preferable to apply the rule relating to instantaneous modes (see above), i.e. that the contract will not come into being until the acceptance has been received. This was accepted by Blair J in *Thomas v BPE Solicitors (A Firm)*, 2010.

There is then the issue of precisely when the message can be said to have been received; is it when the message is transmitted to the server; to the offeror's computer (or within a reasonable time thereafter); or when it is actually read. Given the practical problems that may arise, the second of these three possibilities would appear to be the most sensible.

Acceptance Must Be Given in Exchange for the Offer

Where there is an offer of the unilateral type, the question arises as to whether there is a contract where a person fulfils the condition contained in the offer without knowledge that the offer has been made.

In the American case of *Fitch v Snedaker*, 1868, it was ruled that a person who gives information without knowledge of the offer of a reward cannot claim the reward. In the Australian case, *R. v Clarke*, 1927, the principle was extended to the case of a person who had once known of the offer but at the time of the purported acceptance it had "passed from his mind". Despite the apparently contrary decision in *Gibbons v Proctor*, 1891, English law is thought to be in accordance with Fitch's case. Motive, however, is not relevant; in *Williams v Carwardine*, 1833, it was held that the claimant was entitled to a reward even though she gave the information out of a motive of spite.

A similar problem is that of identical cross-offers, i.e. where A offers to sell and Y offers to buy the same goods on the same terms, each offer being made in ignorance of the other, the offers crossing in the post. It is thought that no contract would be formed on these facts as there is no true offer and acceptance; *Tinn v Hoffman*, 1873.

TERMINATION OF OFFER

Unless accepted, an offer has no legal effect. Apart from counter-offer (already discussed) and express rejection, an offer may terminate in the following ways.

Revocation

An offer may be revoked at any time until it is accepted. In *Routledge v Grant*, 1828, it was held that a promise to keep the offer open for a period of time will not be binding unless supported by consideration (see Chapter 4). Further, revocation will only be effective if communicated to the offeree. Thus, in *Byrne v Van Tienhoven*, 1880, the defendants made an offer to the claimants by letter on October 1. The claimants received the letter on October 11, and immediately accepted by telegram. Meanwhile on October 8, the defendants had sent a letter revoking their offer, which arrived on October 20. It was held there was a binding contract since revocation was ineffective until communicated but acceptance was effective as from October 11.

Communication of revocation need not be made by the offeror personally; it may be sufficient if revocation is communicated by some reliable third party; *Dickinson v Dodds*, CA, 1876. Where the offer is made to the public at large, as in a unilateral contract, it may be validly revoked by taking reasonable steps to notify persons who might be likely to accept; *Shuey v US*, 1875.

In unilateral contracts, where acceptance is denoted by the performance of some stipulated act, the question arises as to when acceptance is effective so as to prevent the offeror from revoking, i.e. at the commencement or on completion of the act. Various solutions have been advanced but the general rule would seem to be, as a result of *Offord v Davis*, 1862 and in the key case discussed below that, once the offeree has commenced performance, the offeror may not revoke.

ERRINGTON V ERRINGTON, CA, 1952

A father financed the purchase of a house by mortgage, and allowed his daughter and son-in-law to live in it, on terms that if they paid off all the mortgage repayments, the house would be theirs. The couple made no counter-promise and so the contract was unilateral.

Held: Once the couple commenced and continued making the repayments, the offer could not be revoked. However, the father would not be liable on his promise until performance of the stipulated act was complete; i.e. when all the repayments were made.

Comment

In *Daulia Ltd v Four Millbank Nominees Ltd*, CA, 1978, the Court of Appeal, obiter, accepted the above analysis. The rule stated in Errington is a general one and will not be applied where it is contrary to the parties' intentions, e.g. in estate agency commission agreements; *Luxor (Eastbourne) Ltd v Cooper*, HL, 1941.

Figure 3: Byrne v Van Tienhoven

| STAGE 1: Defendants posted offer |
| STAGE 2: Defendants posted revocation |
| STAGE 3: Claimants received offer and telegraphed acceptance |
| STAGE 4: Claimants received revocation |

Binding contract: postal rule applies at Stage 3.

Lapse

An offer will lapse either after a fixed period for which it has been left open, or, in the absence of a fixed period, after a reasonable length of time has passed. What is reasonable will depend upon the circumstances of the offer and the subject matter; thus an offer to buy perishable goods or a commodity where the price fluctuates daily will lapse fairly quickly. In *Ramsgate Victoria Hotel v Montefiore*, 1866, an offer to buy shares could not be accepted after the expiry of five months from when it was made; the offer was held to have lapsed.

An offer may also lapse if it is made subject to a condition which then fails. In *Financings Ltd v Stimson*, CA, 1962, an offer to sell a car on hire-purchase was held to be subject to an implied condition that the car remained undamaged until the moment of acceptance. As this condition had been broken, there was no contract.

Death

If the offeror dies before acceptance, there is authority that the offeree may validly accept providing: (i) it is not a contract involving the personal service of the offeror; and (ii) the offeree has not been notified of the death; *Bradbury v Morgan*, 1862.

There is, however, a dictum to the contrary in *Dickinson v Dodds*, CA, 1876, per Mellish LJ: "... if a man who makes an offer dies, the offer cannot be accepted after he is dead".

If the offeree dies before acceptance, then it seems the offer will terminate and cannot be accepted by his personal representatives.

. . . .

ANOMALOUS CASES

In *Gibson v Manchester CC*, HL, 1979, the House of Lords recognised that there may be certain exceptional types of case where, although it is clear that the parties have reached agreement, it is difficult to discern an offer and acceptance. An example is *Clarke v Dunraven*, HL, 1897, where the rules of a yacht club were held to form the basis of a binding contract between each member, one to another, and in *Brogden v Metropolitan Railway*, HL, 1877, the House of Lords inferred a contract from the conduct of the parties although there had been no actual express acceptance as such. The possibility of a contract coming into being during and as a result of performance was confirmed in *G. Percy Trentham Ltd v Archital Luxfer*, CA, 1993; and *RTS Flexible Systems Ltd v Molkerei Alois Mulleer GmbH*, SC, 2010.

REVISION CHECKLIST

You should now know and understand:

☐ the meaning of offer and invitation to treat;

☐ what constitutes the acceptance of an offer;

☐ when the postal rule of acceptance applies;

☐ the various ways in which an offer may be terminated.

QUESTION AND ANSWER

THE QUESTION

Xerxes Plc, who manufacture oil rigs, wrote to Mogul Ltd, an oil company, offering to construct an oil rig for £1,000,000. The offer was made on a form containing Xerxes's standard terms of business. One of the terms contained in the document was that the initially agreed contract price might be varied according to the cost and availability of materials.

Mogul replied, in a letter containing their standard terms of business, stating that they wished to order the rig. These terms did not include a price variation clause but contained a statement that the order was not valid unless confirmed by return of post. Xerxes duly confirmed by a letter dated May 1 which was delayed in the post as it bore the wrong address and did not arrive until May 14.

Meanwhile, on May 12, Mogul posted a letter to Xerxes cancelling the order which arrived on May 13. Xerxes ignored this letter and pressed on with the construction of the rig. It was completed one year later at a price of £2,000,000. Mogul refuse to take delivery.

Advise Mogul Ltd.

ADVICE AND THE ANSWER

General guidance

You can expect that there will be a question on offer and acceptance in the examination (it is a rare examination paper that excludes it altogether) and it is a topic which lends itself to problem-type questions. It is an area where there are a lot of rules, mostly contained in cases, and you will be tested on the interplay between the various rules. For example, the outcome of the question may turn on whether an advertisement is an offer or an invitation to treat; whether there has been a counter-offer or a mere request for information; whether the postal rule applies; or whether or not there has been an effective revocation. The fact that a postal acceptance (where the postal rule applies) is effective on posting may have to be considered against a revocation, which is only effective when it is received. It almost goes without saying that to achieve a good mark, you will need a sound grasp of the case law and the ability to apply the law to the facts.

OFFER AND ACCEPTANCE

Sometimes questions on offer and acceptance incorporate other issues, such as intention to create legal relations or remedies. By way of illustration, in the question above, there is an issue regarding mitigation of loss. You may wish to revisit this point after studying Chapter 14 on remedies.

Model answer

Whether or not Mogul can refuse to take delivery depends upon whether or not there is a binding contract between Xerxes and Mogul. Xerxes made the initial offer on their standard terms of business. As Mogul's reply is on different terms, it would seem to be in the nature of a counter-offer, rather than an acceptance. It was held in *Hyde v Wrench*, 1840, that the effect of a counter-offer is to operate as a rejection of the original offer. However, the counter-offer is itself an offer and may be accepted on its own terms.

The problem here is often referred to as the "battle of the forms". Although it has been argued that, in this situation, the contract should be concluded on the original offeror's terms as the offeree, by purporting to accept, waives his own terms, the Court of Appeal in *Butler Machine Tool Co Ltd v Ex-Cell-O Corp*, CA, 1979 preferred to adopt the traditional view that the offeree in such a situation makes a counter-offer.

The next question is whether Mogul's counter-offer has been accepted by Xerxes. The general rule is that acceptance must be communicated. If Xerxes's letter of confirmation was only effective when communicated, i.e. when it arrived on May 14, there would be no contract because the counter-offer would have been revoked by Mogul's letter of cancellation which arrived on May 13. Revocation is effective when communicated; *Byrne Co v Van Tienhoven Co*, 1880. However, where the post is the proper means of communication between the parties, a letter of acceptance is effective immediately it is posted even if delayed or lost; Household Fire, etc., *Insurance Co v Grant*, 1879. If the postal rule of acceptance were to apply here, the contract would be concluded on the date of posting which we may take to be May 1 and Mogul's purported revocation would be ineffective.

On the facts, there is reason to question whether the postal rule of acceptance would apply. First, it is possible to argue that the wording of the counter-offer ("confirm by return of post") might be construed as requiring actual communication to arrive within a short period. In *Holwell Securities v Hughes*, CA, 1974, an offer to sell land stipulated that acceptance should be "by notice in writing". It was held that the form of the words excluded the postal rule of acceptance. In this case, everything would depend upon the interpretation placed by the court on the words used. Secondly, the letter of acceptance was delayed because it was misaddressed. Although there is no authority directly on the point, it is thought that if the misdirection is due to the offeree's carelessness, the postal rule of acceptance will not apply. This is suggested by the analogous case of *Getreideimport GmbH v Contimar*, 1953. Nevertheless, the misdirection could be the fault of the offeror, e.g. in supplying the wrong address. In such a case, Treitel (Law of Contract) has suggested that the true rule is that a misdirected acceptance takes effect (if at all) at the time which is least favourable to the party responsible for misdirection. In this case, if the fault were traceable to Mogul, the postal rule of acceptance might be held to apply. Treitel's view has been confirmed, obiter, in *Korbetis v Transgrain Shipping BV*, 2005.

If the contract is binding due to a valid postal acceptance, Mogul's letter of May 12 could be regarded as a repudiatory breach of contract. Xerxes are not bound to accept the repudiation, and in the circumstances are under no duty to mitigate. On the authority of *White and Carter (Councils) Ltd v McGregor*, HL, 1962, Xerxes would be entitled to complete performance and claim the contractual sum due, which would presumably be £1,000,000 as the price variation clause is excluded from the contract. However, this principle is subject to the limitation that it will not apply where the claimant has no substantial or legitimate interest in completing performance rather than claiming damages (per Lord Reid in White and Carter.) It is conceivable that a manufacturer of large capital goods could have such an interest, though the position may ultimately depend on whether Xerxes have acted wholly unreasonably in completing performance rather than claiming damages; Attica Sea Carriers Case, CA, 1976; and *Isabella Shipowner SA v Shagang Shipping Co Ltd*, 2012.

It would seem that Mogul's best hope is to show that no contract was concluded.

Intention to be Legally Bound

INTRODUCTION

The intention to be legally bound is an essential element of a binding contract. As a general principle:

(a) Domestic and social agreements are presumed not to be intended to be legally binding.

(b) In commercial agreements there is a strong presumption that the parties intend to be legally bound.

The courts have recognised that some agreements, by their very nature, are not intended to be legally binding and in others the parties may expressly declare or indicate that they do not intend to assume contractual relations.

The case law in this area establishes that, despite doubts expressed by some academic commentators, the intention to contract is a necessary independent element in the formation of a contract. The cases may be classified under five headings.

ADVERTISEMENTS

For the purpose of attracting custom, tradesmen may make vague exaggerated claims in advertisements. Such statements are essentially statements of opinion or "mere puff" and are not intended to form the basis of a binding contract. It should be noted, however, that even a precise statement will not be binding if it is clear that it was not seriously meant; in *Weeks v Tybald*, 1605, the defendant was not bound when he offered £100 to the man who would marry his daughter with his consent.

Even in advertisements, the court will look for evidence of contractual intent, thus in Carlill's case (see Chapter 2), the company's defence that their advertisement was mere puff was rejected by the court on the ground that the company had deposited £1,000 in a bank as proof of their sincerity.

DOMESTIC AGREEMENTS

> ## KEY CASE
>
> BALFOUR V BALFOUR, ca, 1919
> A husband who was posted abroad, leaving his wife to stay in England due to ill-health, promised to pay her a monthly allowance. The husband failed to pay and the wife sought payment.
>
> **Held:** Agreements of a domestic nature between a husband and wife living together as one household are presumed *not* to be intended to be legally binding, unless the agreement states to the contrary.
>
> ### Comment
> The presumption against contractual intention will not apply where the spouses are not living together in amity at the time of the agreement, as in *Merritt v Merritt*, CA, 1969, where the parties had separated by the time they made their agreement.

It seems that agreements of a domestic nature between parent and child are likewise presumed not to be intended to be binding; *Jones v Padavatton*, CA, 1969. Where the parties to the agreement share a household but are not related, the court will examine all the circumstances; in *Simpkins v Pays*, 1955, an agreement between the members of a household to share the winnings of a competition they jointly entered was held to be legally binding.

Where members of a family have a business relationship with each other there will be contractual intention in relation to contracts of a business, as opposed to a domestic, nature; *Snelling v John G. Snelling Ltd*, 1972.

SOCIAL AGREEMENTS

It is recognised that there is a sphere of social arrangements where contractual relations are not intended; "To offer a friend a meal is not to invite litigation": Cheshire, Fifoot and Furmston, *Law of Contract*. This presumption against contractual intention has been applied by the courts to a variety of arrangements including a golf competition (*Lens v The Devonshire Club*, 1914) and to an arrangement for sharing petrol costs where a person is given a lift to work; *Coward v Motor Insurers' Bureau*, CA, 1963. In neither case was there held to be a contract. It seems that where an agreement to share lottery winnings between friends is alleged, a sufficiently certain antecedent agreement is required; *Wilson v Burnett*, 2007.

COMMERCIAL AGREEMENTS

CHECKPOINT

Commercial agreements—in such agreements, there is a strong presumption that the parties intend to be legally bound.

This presumption may generally only be rebutted by express words, as in the key case below.

KEY CASE

ROSE AND FRANK CO V CROMPTON BROS. LTD, HL, 1925
The appellants, an American firm, signed a document with an English company (the respondents) appointing the appellants sole agents of the respondents to sell their products in the USA. The document contained an "honourable pledge clause" which provided that the sole agency agreement should not be subject to the legal jurisdiction of the law courts. The respondents later ended the agreement and the appellants sued.

Held: The usual presumption that commercial agreements are legally binding was rebutted by the clear words used. However, individual orders given and accepted were enforceable contracts, based on the parties' conduct.

Comment
It may be asked, why is the honourable pledge clause binding on the parties if there is no binding contract as stated by the clause itself? Although it seems illogical that the clause should be binding, perhaps the answer lies in the pragmatic readiness of the courts to give effect to the clear intentions of the parties.

Similarly, football pools stated to be "binding in honour only" are not legal contracts so that a participant may not recover the winnings; *Jones v Vernon's Pools*, 1938.

The onus of rebutting contractual intent is a heavy one; in *Edwards v Skyways Ltd*, 1964 a redundancy agreement providing for an ex gratia payment to be made to an employee was held to be a binding contract; the expression used was insufficient to rebut contractual intention. *Esso Petroleum Ltd v Commissioners of Customs and Excise*, HL, 1976 shows the difficulty of rebutting contractual intention where clear words are not used. Esso distributed World Cup coins to be given free to any motorist who purchased a specified amount of petrol. The House of Lords was divided on the issue of contractual intention.

In *Kleinwort Benson Ltd v Malaysia Mining Corp*, CA, 1989, it was held that a "letter of comfort", where a company stated that it was its policy to ensure that its subsidiary could meet its liability in respect of loans made to it, did not have contractual effect. The words in question were intended as a statement of existing fact and not as a contractual promise.

The issue of intention arose in *Edmonds v Lawson*, CA, 2000. A pupil barrister contended that pupillage constituted a "contract of employment" under s.54(3)(a) of the National Minimum Wage Act 1998. Even though pupils are generally unpaid, the Court of Appeal held that there was an intention to create legal relations. Pupils provided consideration for the offer made by chambers by agreeing to enter the productive relationship which pupillage involved. However, pupillage was not a contract of apprenticeship and the claimant was not a "worker" within the meaning of the 1998 Act. There was therefore no entitlement to receive the national minimum wage.

Where the agreement falls between the commercial and social, the onus is on the claimant to prove contractual intention, although the onus is less heavy than in a purely social context; *Sadler v Reynolds*, 2005.

COLLECTIVE AGREEMENTS

A collective agreement is an agreement between a trade union and an employer regulating rates of pay and conditions of work. If the terms of such an agreement are incorporated into an individual employee's contract of service, they will be legally binding on the parties. With regard to the agreement itself, the position at common law was that collective agreements were not intended to be legally binding between union and employer; *Ford Motor Co Ltd v A.U.E.F.W.*, 1969.

The position at common law has been affirmed by statute: under s.179(1) and (2) of the Trade Union and Labour Relations (Consolidation) Act 1992, a collective agreement is presumed not to have been intended by the parties to be a legally enforceable contract unless it is in writing and expressly provides to the contrary.

Figure 4: Intention to be Legally Bound

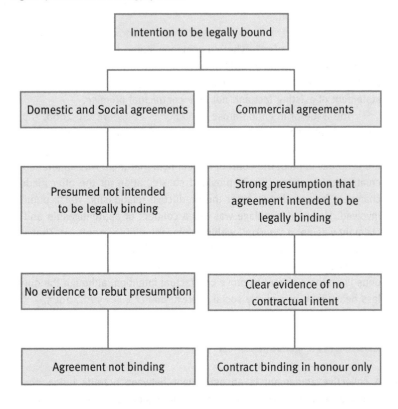

REVISION CHECKLIST

You should now know and understand:

☐ what is required in order to rebut the presumption that domestic agreements are not intended to be binding;

☐ the circumstances in which the presumption that commercial agreements are intended to be binding may be rebutted.

QUESTION AND ANSWER

"All contracts are agreements, but not all agreements are contracts."

Discuss in relation to the requirement of contractual intention in the formation of contract.

ADVICE AND THE ANSWER

General guidance

The topic of intention to be legally bound often appears as an issue in a question which deals also with other aspects of formation of contract, such as offer and acceptance or consideration. For example, it might be the case that the parties to a consideration problem are relatives or friends. This would raise the issue that, even if there was consideration, the agreement might not be enforceable as being a domestic or social agreement where there is a presumption against legal relations. One would then look for factors to rebut the presumption, such as whether the agreement has been committed to writing and is in certain terms or, whether there has been performance under the agreement.

The above question is a relatively rare example of a question that predominantly concentrates on the topic of intention. The quotation is slightly cryptic, and as with all essay-type questions, one should be wary of attempting the question in an examination unless one is sure of what it is about. Essentially, the proposition is that there are some agreements which lack contractual force because some element is missing. The rubric indicates that the element is intention.

Answer plan

1 An answer should begin by observing that intention is one of the three essential elements of a binding contract, along with offer and acceptance (i.e. agreement) and consideration.

2 A good answer might observe that this proposition has been questioned by some commentators who argue that as a contract is a bargain, offer, acceptance and consideration will suffice and the test of intention is superfluous and artificial. This is not the position in law, however, as the decided cases demonstrate.

INTENTION TO BE LEGALLY BOUND

27

3 Domestic agreements should then be analysed. In *Balfour v Balfour*, CA, 1919 an agreement between a husband and wife relating to a monthly allowance was held to be legally unenforceable owing to a lack of intent. There was a presumption that the parties did not intend to be legally bound; they were living together in amity at the time of the agreement.

4 Lord Atkin observed that agreements such as these are outside the realm of the courts altogether; if such agreements were enforceable then "the small courts of this country would have to be multiplied one hundredfold". There may be an underlying policy consideration here that the courts should not become involved with family relationships and that, if they did, the floodgates of litigation would open.

5 Of course, where the parties are separated at the time of the agreement, the position may be different as in *Merritt v Merritt*, CA, 1969. Here a married couple separated and then at a subsequent meeting the husband promised that if the wife would pay off the mortgage, he would convey the matrimonial home to her. The transaction was held binding, the presumption against contractual relation was rebutted. The fact that the terms of the agreement were recorded in a written document was important because it provided a degree of certainty that such agreements may lack.

6 The answer should then go on to analyse further examples of domestic relationships, thus in *Jones v Padavatton*, CA, 1969, the court confirmed that the *Balfour v Balfour* principles apply to other domestic relationships such as parent and child. Here a mother was held entitled to possession of a house that she had bought for her daughter to live in whilst the daughter was a law student.

7 In *Simpkins v Pays*, 1955, however, where members of a household (some of whom were not related to each other) shared the costs of entering a weekly competition, the court examined all the circumstances and concluded that there was an intention to be bound.

8 There are two further situations where there it is generally understood that the parties do not intend contractual relations: these are
    (i)   advertisements; and
    (ii) social agreements.
In the former, statements made by advertisers are generally treated as "mere puff"; in the case of the latter, the courts are reluctant to find a contract—"to offer a friend a meal is not to invite litigation".

9 When it comes to commercial agreements, the presumption is the other way, i.e. there is a strong presumption that the parties intend contractual relations. If the presumption is to be rebutted, it requires a very clear express provision in the contract; e.g. *Rose and Frank Co v*

Crompton Bros. Ltd, HL, 1925 (a clearly worded "honour clause" stating that the contract would not be subject to the jurisdiction of the law courts was upheld). The court nevertheless held that where orders had been accepted, there was a legal obligation to deliver.

10 The decision in *Rose and Frank v Crompton* has come in for some criticism. It may be asked: why is the honour clause binding on the parties if there is no binding contract as stated by the clause itself? Nevertheless, honour clauses have been used for many years by football pool companies in their coupons—such a clause was upheld in *Jones v Vernon's Pools*, 1938.

11 The onus of rebutting contractual intent in commercial agreements is a heavy one. In *Edwards v Skyways Ltd*, 1964 the use of the words, "ex gratia" did not rebut the presumption.

12 So-called "letters of comfort" are construed as statements of fact rather than promises which are contractual in nature; *Kleinwort Benson Ltd v Malaysia Mining Corp*, CA, 1989.

13 By way of conclusion, it might well be asserted with some justification that not all agreements are contracts in the sense of being legally binding.

Consideration

INTRODUCTION

To be binding a simple contract must be supported by consideration. This chapter is concerned with what is meant by "valuable consideration" in the law of contract. It involves an examination of the following:

1 The definition of consideration
2 The meaning of "past" consideration
3 The rule that consideration must move from the promisee
4 Whether consideration is provided by the performance of, or the promise to perform, a duty already owed
5 The part-payment of debts
6 The circumstances in which promissory estoppel applies

In addition to offer and acceptance and contractual intent, consideration is an essential element in the formation of any contract not by deed.

English law will not enforce a gratuitous or "bare" promise. By way of example, if one party, A (the promisor), promises to mow the lawn of another, B (the promisee), A's promise will only be enforceable by B as a contract if B has provided consideration. The consideration from B might normally take the form of a payment of money but could consist of some other service to which A might agree. Further, the promise of a money payment or service in the future is just as sufficient a consideration as payment itself or the actual rendering of the service. Thus, the promisee has to give something in return for the promise of the promisor in order to convert a bare promise made in his favour into a binding contract.

CHECKPOINT

Consideration has been defined in terms of: "an act or forbearance of one party, or the promise thereof, is the price for which the promise of the other is bought, and the promise thus given for value is enforceable" (Pollock, approved by Lord Dunedin in *Dunlop Pneumatic Tyre Co v Selfridge Ltd*, HL, 1915). It follows that English law requires a simple contract to be a *bargain* and this aspect is stressed in the above definition.

Another definition (given by Lush J in *Currie v Misa*, 1875) refers to consideration as consisting of a detriment to the promisee or a benefit to the promisor:

> "[S]ome right, interest, profit or benefit accruing to the one party, or some forbearance, detriment, loss or responsibility given, suffered or undertaken by the other."

It should be noted that the words "benefit" and "detriment" do not refer to whether or not the bargain is an advantageous one; thus a person who, in return for a money payment, promises to abstain from smoking will legally incur a detriment and provide consideration even though the promise is beneficial to his health. If he has never smoked anyway then it is doubtful whether he could be said to incur a detriment; see *Arrale v Costain Civil Engineering Ltd*, 1975.

The definition of Lush J referred to above speaks of benefit and detriment as alternatives; it might be more accurate to say that whilst consideration may consist of a benefit to the promisor, it must always consist of a detriment to the promisee because of the rule (discussed below) that consideration must always move from the promisee.

Figure 5: Making a Promise Binding

Binding contract: consideration provided

TYPES OF CONSIDERATION

Consideration is called "executory" where there is an exchange of promises to perform acts in the future, e.g. a bilateral contract for the supply of goods whereby A promises to deliver goods to B at a future date and B promises to pay on delivery. Alternatively, consideration is referred to as "executed" where one party performs an act in fulfilment of a promise made by the other, e.g. the unilateral contract where A offers a reward to anyone who provides certain information. Both these types of consideration should be distinguished from "past" consideration which is discussed below.

JUDICIAL RULES RELATING TO CONSIDERATION

The courts have developed certain technical rules in relation to consideration. These are detailed below.

Consideration Must Not be Past

Past consideration, unlike executory or executed consideration, is not good or valid consideration. Consideration is said to be past when it consists of some service or benefit previously rendered to the promisor. Whether consideration is past is a question of fact.

KEY CASE

RE MCARDLE, CA, 1951
A woman carried out work to a house jointly owned by members of her family. After the work had been completed, her relatives signed a document promising to pay her for the work. They did not pay.

Held: She could not recover the sum promised as her consideration was past.

Comment
It made no difference that the promise was embodied in a signed document having all the appearance of a "contract". Nothing had been given in return for the promise—there was no exchange and so no consideration.

The Requested Performance Exception

If, however, the service is performed at the defendant's request and in circumstances where both parties understand that payment will follow, the court may be prepared to enforce the transaction: *Lampleigh v Braithwait*, 1615; *Kennedy v Broun*, 1863. Thus, if, in *Re McArdle*, the woman had been first requested by her relatives to carry out the work, the consideration may not have been regarded as past. The law on this point is substantially contained in *Re Casey's Patents*, *Stewart v Casey*, CA, 1892. Patent owners wrote to their manager, "in consideration of your (past) services ... as manager", they would give him a one-third share. The Court of Appeal rejected the patent owners' submission that the services were past consideration. The original request being implied, the performance of the services had raised an implication that they would be paid for and the subsequent express promise to pay merely fixed the amount. This decision was affirmed by the Privy Council in *Pau On v Lau Yiu Long*, PC, 1980.

Here, Lord Scarman identified three essentials if the requested performance exception is to apply:

(i)   the act must have been done at the promisor's request;

(ii) the parties *must have understood throughout* that the act was to be remunerated either by payment or the conferment of some other benefit; and

(iii) payment, or the conferment of a benefit, must have been legally enforceable had it been promised in advance.

Two statutory exceptions to the rule about past consideration should be noted:

(1) Section 27 of the Bills of Exchange Act 1882 provides that an antecedent debt or liability will support a bill of exchange; and

(2) Sections 29 and 30 of the Limitation Act 1980 provide that where a debt is acknowledged within the statutory limitation period, the limitation period begins to run again from the date of acknowledgment.

Figure 6: Requested Performance Exception

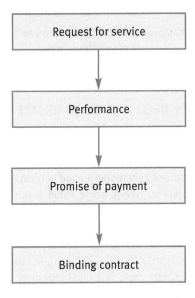

Consideration Must Move from the Promisee

Only a person who has provided consideration in return for a promise may enforce that promise as a contract. In *Tweddle v Atkinson*, 1861, X agreed with Y that they would each pay a sum to X's son Z, who was Y's prospective son-in-law. Z's action against Y's executors failed as no consideration had moved from Z.

It may well be thought that the principle in the above case is in effect the same principle as the rule of "privity of contract", however, the courts have treated them as distinct. It should be noted that under the provisions of the Contracts (Rights of Third Parties) Act 1999, a third party who can bring him or herself within the terms of the legislation may well have an enforceable action in cases such as *Tweddle v Atkinson* (see Chapter 12).

Figure 7: Tweddle v Atkinson

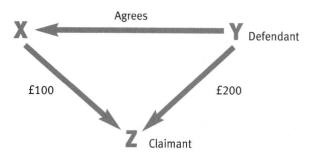

Z has provided no consideration and cannot
enforce the contract

CONSIDERATION NEED NOT BE ADEQUATE

Providing consideration has some value, the courts will not investigate its adequacy. A contract is a bargain freely entered into and the courts are not concerned with whether it constitutes a good bargain. Where consideration is recognised by the law as having some value it is described as "real" or "sufficient" consideration. For example, a rent of £1 per annum (a "peppercorn" rent) would be sufficient consideration for the grant of lease on premises worth thousands, providing, of course, the transaction was entered into freely. In *Chappell & Co Ltd v Nestle Co Ltd*, HL, 1960, the House of Lords considered, in a copyright case, that used chocolate wrappers were part of the consideration for the purchase of a gramophone record. Similar examples of relatively trivial but sufficient consideration include the promise to surrender a document believed to be valuable but in fact of no legal effect (*Haigh v Brooks*, 1839); the temporary and apparently purposeless deprivation of a chattel (*Bainbridge v Firmstone*, 1838) and the possibility that the publication of a letter in a newspaper might increase the paper's circulation; *De La Bere v Pearson Ltd*, CA, 1908.

Illusory Consideration

We have seen that, in order to be sufficient, consideration must have some value, however trivial. However, if the consideration is empty or illusory, or concerned with sentiment or human feelings, the courts have tended to regard it as insufficient. It is sometimes said that consideration must have some "economic" value, though this formulation is perhaps a little narrow. In *White v Bluett*, 1853, a son's promise not to bore his father with complaints was held not to be sufficient consideration for a promise by the father to discharge the son's debts; in *Thomas v Thomas*, 1842, a husband's desire that his widow should live in his house after his death was held not to be part of the consideration for the executor's promise that she could do so. *Eastwood v Kenyon*, 1840 is a similar decision where the court refused to recognise a moral obligation as a sufficient consideration to enforce a promise to pay a sum of money.

Another group of cases where consideration has been held to be insufficient is where it consists of a promise to perform, or the performance of, some existing duty already owed by the promisee to the promisor, either as a result of some public duty or under an existing contract with the promisor. These cases will be dealt with below.

Existing Public Duty

Collins v Godefroy, 1831 is usually cited as authority for the proposition that the performance of an existing public duty is not consideration. In that case, the defendant promised to pay the claimant a sum of money for giving evidence in a court action in which the claimant had been subpoenaed. As the claimant was under a legal duty to attend court, it was held that he had not furnished consideration. There are, however, suggestions in other cases (e.g. *Morgan v Palmer*, 1824) that the real reason for the law refusing to enforce such contracts is that they are contrary to public policy.

Consideration will be furnished when an existing public duty is exceeded. Thus, if the police agree to provide a colliery with extra protection during a miners' strike, they provide consideration for a promise to pay them for that extra service; *Glasbrook Bros v Glamorgan CC*, HL, 1925. In *Ward v Byham*, CA, 1956, the mother of an illegitimate child promised the father, in return for a weekly allowance, that she would keep the child "well looked-after and happy". It was held, by the majority of the Court of Appeal, that the mother had provided consideration in that she had promised to exceed her statutory duty, which was merely to "maintain" the child (cf. *White v Bluett* (above)). Lord Denning, in this case, thought the agreement enforceable, but on the unorthodox ground that a promise to perform an existing duty is good consideration as it is a benefit to the person to whom it is given.

Existing Contractual Duty

The rule here is that the performance of an existing contractual duty owed to the promisor is not sufficient consideration. Authority for the principle is to be found in the following case.

KEY CASE

STILK V MYRICK, 1809
Two sailors deserted a ship and the captain promised the remaining eight crew members extra wages if they would work the ship home. They were already bound to do this under their contracts.

Held: The captain's promise was not binding.

Comment
The reports of the case reveal two bases for the decision:
  (i) that the crew had given no consideration, as they were already bound to meet the foreseeable emergencies of the voyage and work the ship home; and
  (ii) that the promise could not be enforced as it was contrary to public policy.
The lack of consideration theory receives modern support from *Swain v West (Butchers) Ltd*, 1936 and *North Ocean Shipping Co Ltd v Hyundai Construction Co Ltd*, 1979 although that decision was based on economic duress (see Chapter 10).

In *Hartley v Ponsonby*, 1857 it was held, in another "seamen's wages" case, that there was consideration for the promise to pay extra wages. The desertion of half the crew had rendered the ship short-handed and so the voyage became more dangerous. Existing contractual duty had been exceeded and effectively a fresh bargain had been entered into.

A "qualification" to *Stilk v Myrick* has been introduced whereby if the performance of an existing contractual duty confers a practical benefit on the other party this can constitute valid consideration, as in the case below.

KEY CASE

WILLIAMS V ROFFEY BROS AND NICHOLLS (CONTRACTORS) LTD, CA, 1990
The defendants were building contractors refurbishing 27 flats. They contracted with the claimant to carry out joinery work for £20,000. The defendants' main contract contained a time penalty clause and they were concerned that the claimant would not complete the work on time. Consequently, the defendants promised to pay the claimant a

£10,300 bonus if he completed on time. The claimant carried out the work but the defendants did not pay the bonus.

Held: The claimant had provided consideration by completing the work on time. Glidewell LJ ruled that:

(1) if A has entered into a contract with B to do work for, or supply goods and services to, B in return for payment by B; and

(2) at some stage before A has completely performed his obligations under the contract, B has reason to doubt whether A will, or will be able to, complete his side of the bargain; and

(3) B thereupon promises A an additional payment in return for A's promise to perform his contractual obligations on time; and

(4) as a result of giving his promise, B obtains in practice a benefit, or obviates a disbenefit; and

(5) B's promise is not given as a result of economic duress or fraud on the part of A; then

(6) the benefit to B is capable of being consideration for B's promise, so that the promise will be legally binding.

Comment

In *South Carribean Trading v Trafigura Beheer BV*, 2005, the court strenuously criticised the reasoning on which *Williams v Roffey* is based—it was considered to be "inconsistent" with the rule that consideration, being the price of the promise, must move from the promisee.

Existing Contractual Duty Owed to a Third Party

There is clear authority that the performance, or the promise to perform, an existing contractual duty owed by the promisee to a third party, is good consideration.

In *Scotson v Pegg*, 1861, A agreed to deliver coal to B, or to B's order. B ordered A to deliver the coal to C. C promised A that if A would deliver the coal, he would unload it. In an action by A to enforce C's promise, it was held that A's delivery of the coal (the performance of an existing contractual duty to a third party, B) was good consideration to enforce C's promise.

Further support for the existence of the rule is to be found in *Shadwell v Shadwell*, 1860. Here the claimant wrote to his nephew congratulating him on his engagement to a young woman called Ellen Nichol and promised to pay him £150 per annum until such time as he was earning 600 guineas as a Chancery barrister. The claimant married but the uncle's executors refused to pay. It was held that although the claimant was already bound by his promise to marry, the claimant had provided consideration in that he had suffered a detriment—he had incurred financial liabilities in reliance on the uncle's promise. Further, the marriage was a benefit to the uncle because it was "an object of interest" with a near relative. (It should be noted that an engagement to marry was a contractually binding commitment at the time.)

Two modern Privy Council decisions expressly approve *Scotson v Pegg*. These are *New Zealand Shipping Co Ltd v A.M. Satterthwaite Co Ltd*, PC, 1975 and *Pau On v Lau Yiu Long*, PC, 1980, as a result of which it would seem that the principle relating to existing contractual duty owed to a third party is firmly established.

Figure 8: Shadwell v Shadwell

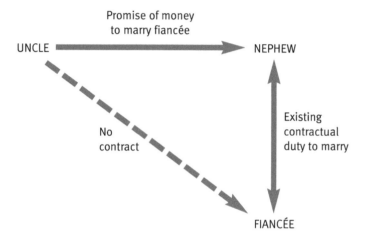

Nephew provides consideration by marrying fiancée

PART-PAYMENT OF DEBTS

The discharge of debts gives rise to certain problems concerning consideration.

The rule at common law (the rule in Pinnel's case, 1602) is that the part-payment of a debt is not good consideration for a promise to forgo the balance. Thus, if A owes B £50 and B accepts £25 in full satisfaction on the due date, there is nothing to prevent B from claiming the balance at a later date, since there is no consideration proceeding from A to enforce the promise of B to accept part payment. However, it was held in Pinnel's case that the agreement to accept part-payment would be binding if A, at B's request, provided some fresh consideration. Consideration might be provided if:

(1) B agrees to accept part-payment on an earlier date than the due date (i.e. as in Pinnel's case itself); or

(2) B agrees to accept a chattel instead of money (even if worth less than the debt since consideration need not be adequate); or

(3) B agrees to accept part-payment in a different place to that originally specified.

Until 1966 it used to be the rule that part-payment by cheque, as opposed to notes and coins, was sufficient consideration to discharge a debt. As a result of *D. and C. Builders v Rees*, CA, 1966, overruling earlier cases, the position is now that part payment by cheque does not, without more, discharge a debt.

Despite its harshness and lack of commercial reality, the rule in Pinnel's case was affirmed by the House of Lords in *Foakes v Beer*, HL, 1884 and still represents the law. It is, however, subject to a possible exception in equity, to be discussed below ("promissory estoppel"). The rule was considered in *Re Selectmove*, CA, 1995 where the court declined to extend the principle in *Williams v Roffey* (see above) to the part-payment of debts. Peter Gibson LJ considered that such an extension would in effect leave the principle in *Foakes v Beer* without any application.

There are two exceptions at common law to the rule in Pinnel's case:

(1) Composition agreements. Here a group of creditors who are owed money by a single debtor agree to accept, say, 50p in the pound in absolute discharge. Despite the absence of consideration, it is established that no individual creditor can subsequently sue the debtor for the balance owed to him; *Wood v Robarts*, 1818. The reason usually advanced for the rule is essentially a "policy" one, that to allow an individual creditor to claim the balance would amount to a fraud on the other creditors.

(2) Part-payment of the debt by a third party. If accepted by the creditor in full settlement, part-payment by a third party affords a defence in an action by the creditor to recover the balance. In *Welby v Drake*, 1825 the defendant was indebted to the claimant. The claimant agreed with the defendant's father to accept part-payment by the father in full satisfaction of his son's debt. The money having been paid, it was held that the claimant could not recover the balance from the defendant, as by suing the defendant son, he would commit a fraud on the father.

However, in *Collier v P & MJ Wright (Holdings) Ltd*, CA, 2007 it was held that the mere fact that a creditor agrees with a joint debtor to accept part-payment from him alone of his proportionate share does not amount to a further exception to the rule in Pinnel's case.

PROMISSORY ESTOPPEL

A further, and controversial, exception to the rule in Pinnel's case is to be found in the equitable doctrine of promissory estoppel. The doctrine provides a means of making a promise binding, in certain circumstances, in the absence of consideration.

The modern doctrine is largely based on dicta of Denning J in *Central London Property Trust Ltd v High Trees House Ltd*, 1947, and on the decision of the House of Lords in *Tool Metal Manufacturing Co Ltd v Tungsten Electric Co Ltd*, HL, 1955 and can be traced to the following key case.

KEY CASE

HUGHES V METROPOLITAN RAILWAY, HL, 1877

A landlord gave his tenant six months' notice to repair and in the event of a failure to repair, the lease would be forfeited. Within the six months, the landlord opened negotiations with the tenant for the sale of the lease, during which time the tenant carried out no repairs. Shortly after, negotiations broke down and, at the end of the six-month notice period, the landlord claimed to forfeit the lease.

Held: The landlord could not do so. The landlord had, by his conduct, led the tenant to suppose that the landlord would not enforce forfeiture at the end of the notice period and the tenant had relied on this by not carrying out repairs. However, the six-month period would begin to run again from the date of the breakdown of negotiations.

Comment

The doctrine in *Hughes* is, in effect, a form of equitable or "promissory" estoppel with less strict requirements than common law estoppel which could only arise from a representation of existing fact and not from a promise as to future conduct or intention; *Jorden v Money*, HL, 1854.

The doctrine operates where there has been a representation by one party (the promisor) that they do not intend to enforce their strict legal rights, made with the intention that the other party (the promisee) will rely on the representation, and the other party does in fact rely upon the representation without providing consideration. The party making the representation will be estopped from enforcing his or her strict legal rights, in so far as it is inequitable to do so.

Hughes v Metropolitan Railway was relied on in the key case below.

CENTRAL LONDON PROPERTY TRUST LTD V HIGH TREES HOUSE LTD, 1947
Landlords of a block of flats agreed to accept from the tenants half the
ground rent stipulated in the lease because wartime conditions meant
that there was a shortage of sub-tenants.

Held: By Denning J that by the end of the war the landlords were
entitled to the full rent as the circumstances which gave rise to the rent
reduction were no longer in existence. Despite the absence of consideration, the judge said, obiter, that if the landlords had sought to
recover the balance of rent falling due during the war years, when only
half the rent had been paid, they would have been estopped in equity.

Comment
The *High Trees* case takes the Hughes doctrine perhaps a stage further
as it envisages the extinguishment of the right to receive sums contractually due, i.e. the balance of ground rent.

The exact scope of the doctrine of promissory estoppel is a matter of debate
but it is clear that certain requirements must be satisfied before the doctrine
can come into play:

(1) There must be a clear and unambiguous statement by the promisor
that his or her strict legal rights will not be enforced; *Scandinavian
Trading Tanker Co A.B. v Flota Petrolera Ecuatoriana*, HL, 1983; and *Kim
v Chasewood Park Residents Ltd*, CA, 2013.

(2) The promisee must have acted in reliance on the promise. There is
some uncertainty as to whether the promisee should have relied on the
promise by changing position to their detriment (i.e. so that they are
put in a worse position if the promise is revoked) or whether they
should merely have altered their position in some way, not necessarily
for the worse. In *W. J. Alan Co Ltd v El Nasr Export and Import Co*, CA,
1972, Lord Denning MR said that "he must have been led to act differently from what he otherwise would have done". However, in the
absence of detriment, it might be difficult to show that it is inequitable
for the promisor to go back on his or her word; see (3), below.

(3) It must be inequitable for the promisor to go back on his or her word
and revert to his or her strict legal rights. In *D. and C. Builders v Rees*,
CA, 1966, the debtor took advantage of the creditors' financial straits to
pressure them into accepting part-payment. In an action for the balance of the money owed, Lord Denning MR was of the view that it was
not inequitable for the creditors to go back on their word and claim the

balance as the debtor had acted inequitably by exerting improper pressure.

(4) The doctrine may only be raised as a defence; "as a shield and not a sword". It was held in *Combe v Combe*, CA, 1951 that the doctrine cannot be raised as a cause of action and therefore it does not dispense with the requirement of consideration in the formation of contracts. This decision was affirmed by the Court of Appeal in *Baird Textile Holdings v Marks and Spencer Plc*, CA, 2001. Other common law jurisdictions have been prepared to recognise that promissory estoppel can, in certain circumstances, found a cause of action—this was the conclusion in the Australian case of *Waltons' Stores (Interstate) Ltd v Maher*, 1988. Such a development in English law could now only be instigated by the Supreme Court.

Hitherto, the courts had never conclusively determined whether the doctrine may be applied permanently to extinguish the right to the balance of a lump sum debt after part-payment, or whether it merely suspends the creditor's rights until such time as it is equitable to claim the balance. However, in *Collier v Wright* (for the facts, see preceding section) the court held that the debtor had an arguable case of promissory estoppel. Arden LJ considered that:

> "If (1) a debtor offers to pay part only of the amount he owes; and (2) the creditor voluntarily accepts that offer, and (3) in reliance on the creditor's acceptance the debtor pays part of the amount he owes in full, the creditor will, by virtue of the doctrine of promissory estoppel, be bound to accept that sum in full and final satisfaction of the whole debt."

It seems that, in these circumstances, for the creditor to resile will be inequitable and the estoppel has the effect of extinguishing the creditor's right to the balance of the debt.

Where the debtor's contractual obligation is to make periodic payments, the creditor's right to receive payments during the period of suspension may be permanently extinguished, but the creditor may revert to his or her strict contractual rights either upon giving reasonable notice, or where the circumstances which give rise to the promise have changed (as in *High Trees*). In the *Tool Metal* case, patent owners promised to suspend periodic payments of compensation due to them from manufacturers from the outbreak of war. It was held that the promise was binding during the period of suspension, but the owners could, on giving reasonable notice to the other party, revert to their legal entitlement to receive the compensation payments.

It had always been assumed that promissory estoppel could only arise where there was some contractual or pre-existing legal relationship between the parties. In *Brikom Investments Ltd v Carr*, CA, 1979, Lord Denning MR was of the view that the doctrine can apply to promises made by parties negotiating for a contract, i.e. who are not yet in any legal relationship with each other.

Such an extension of the doctrine is difficult to reconcile with the law relating to pre-contractual representations (see Chapter 6).

REVISION CHECKLIST

You should now know and understand:

- [ ] **the judicial rules relating to consideration;**
- [ ] **the position regarding the part-payment of debts;**
- [ ] **the circumstances in which promissory estoppel may apply.**

QUESTION AND ANSWER

THE QUESTION

Robin is the owner of the Maid Marion Hotel in Nottingley. He wanted to attract more custom to the hotel and so decided to build an indoor swimming pool. He approached the Sheriff Bank to arrange suitable finance for the project.

In March, the Sheriff Bank agreed to loan £120,000 to Robin to be repaid in 12 monthly instalments of £10,000 each plus agreed interest.

Robin contracted with Oak Tree Developments Ltd (OTD) for the pool to be fully constructed and completed by December 1. The noise and disruption caused by the construction meant that hotel bookings were reduced and Robin was soon in financial difficulties. He managed to repay the first six instalments as they fell due but then asked the Sheriff Bank if they would write off the remainder of the debt. This was reluctantly agreed to.

OTD then informed Robin that they might have some difficulty in completing the pool by December 1. Robin promised OTD a bonus of £2,500 if they would "pull out all the stops" and complete the pool on time. Robin also promised every employee of OTD a bonus of £50 each if they got the job done on time.

The pool was in fact completed on time and the hotel attracted a lot of new custom. However, the Sheriff Bank is now demanding that Robin pay the remaining instalments due in respect of the loan as well as all of the arrears. Robin is now refusing to pay any bonuses to either OTD or their employees.

Discuss the legal position.

ADVICE AND THE ANSWER

General guidance

You can expect problem questions on consideration to address the judicial rules relating to consideration—the emphasis will be on whether consideration has been furnished so that there is a binding contract. The rules which most commonly feature include the rules regarding: past consideration, the adequacy of consideration, the rule (in its various forms) that consideration should not consist of a duty already owed, and the principles relating to the part-payment of debts.

Promissory estoppel may also feature. You must remember that this principle only comes into play where there is *no consideration* for a promise. It is important, when considering estoppel, to set out the requirements which must be in place before the doctrine can apply, as in the Model answer below.

Model answer

Sheriff Bank has made a promise not to insist on its strict legal rights. At common law, such promises must be supported by consideration. It was established in Pinnel's case, and confirmed by the House of Lords in *Foakes v Beer*, HL, 1884, that part payment of a debt is not good consideration for a promise to forgo the balance. On this basis the promise of the bank is not binding as Robin has furnished no additional consideration other than that he was originally bound to do.

Although it was held in *Williams v Roffey Bros and Nicholls (Contractors) Ltd*, CA, 1990 that the performance of an existing contractual duty can amount to good consideration if a practical benefit is conferred on the promisor, the Court of Appeal in *Re Selectmove*, CA, 1995 held that the principle in *Williams v Roffey* cannot be extended to debtor-creditor relationships. It seems it must be confined to obligations to supply goods and services—to hold otherwise would undermine the authority of *Foakes v Beer*. Nevertheless, Robin may be able to rely on the doctrine of promissory estoppel. The doctrine was originally enunciated by Lord Cairns L.C. in *Hughes v Metropolitan Railway Co*, HL, 1877 and adopted by Denning J, obiter, in *Central London Property Trust Ltd v High Trees House Ltd*, 1947 who stated that: "the logical consequence [of the doctrine] is that a promise to accept a smaller sum in discharge of a larger sum, if acted upon, is binding notwithstanding the absence of consideration".

The effect of the doctrine is to render binding, despite the lack of consideration, "promises intended to be binding, intended to be acted upon, and in fact acted upon". (Per Denning J)

The doctrine may be relied upon provided certain conditions are satisfied:

1 There must be an existing legal relationship between the parties— Robin and the bank are parties to a loan agreement.

2 The promisor must have made a clear and unequivocal promise not to insist on strict legal rights—the bank has promised to write off the remainder of the debt.

3 The promisee must have altered his position on reliance on the promise. Must the promisee have suffered some detriment as a result of reliance on the promise? Lord Denning has consistently denied this—for example, in *W. J. Alan v El Nasr Export and Import Co*, CA, 1972, he said all that is required is that the promisee has been "led to act differently from what he otherwise would have done".

4 It must be inequitable for the promisor to go back on the promise. Although the presence of detriment may establish such inequity, it may be inequitable to go back on the promise even in the absence of detriment, e.g. as in the *High Trees* case itself. Thus, in the case of Robin, it could be argued that it would be inequitable for the bank to insist on its strict legal rights at least without giving reasonable notice. Further, the promisee must have acted equitably. If Robin's conduct in obtaining the promise amounted to duress then it may not be inequitable for the bank to go back on its promise: *D. and C. Builders v Rees*, CA, 1966.

The traditional view is that the doctrine is merely suspensory (*Hughes v Metropolitan Railway*) and that the strict legal rights of the promisor can be restored on giving reasonable notice: *Tool Metal Manufacturing v Tungsten Electric Co*, HL, 1955. However, Lord Denning considered that the doctrine could extinguish rights and Lord Hodson (in *Ajayi v RT Briscoe*, PC, 1964) accepted that the promise could become "final and irrevocable" if it was impossible for the promisee to resume his position. It could further be argued that where, as here, the obligation of the debtor is to make periodic payments, the effect of "suspension" is only to allow the bank to claim instalments falling due after the expiry of the requisite period of reasonable notice, but not to claim any arrears.

OTD—normally the performance of an existing contractual duty owed to the promisor does not constitute good consideration—*Stilk v Myrick*, 1809. If "pulling out all the stops" could be construed as exceeding the existing contractual duty of OTD, Robin's promise of a bonus may be enforceable—*Hartley v Ponsonby*, 1857. However, this is dubious given the strict contractual obligation of OTD to complete by December 1. Nevertheless, in *Williams v Roffey Bros*, CA 1990, it was held that the performance of an existing contractual duty could, in the absence of duress, amount to good consideration if a practical benefit is conferred on the promisor. In this case it could be argued that Robin has received the practical, as opposed to legal, benefit of the pool being completed on time. It should be noted, however, that unlike in *Williams*, here it is the promisor Robin who is approached by the promisee OTD.

Employees—on the authority of the Privy Council in *New Zealand Shipping Co Ltd v A. M. Satterthwaite Co Ltd*, PC, 1975, it would seem that the performance of an existing contractual duty already owed to a third party can be good consideration despite the absence of additional detriment. Consideration is provided by the acceptance of additional liability. On this basis, the employees would be contractually entitled to the bonus from Robin.

Capacity and Formalities

. . . .

INTRODUCTION

A contract may not be binding on a party if they lack the necessary contractual capacity. In addition, certain types of transaction may not be binding or enforceable if not made in the correct form. In this chapter we are concerned with:

(a) The contractual capacity of corporations; persons of unsound mind and drunkards; and minors.

(b) Those contracts which must be made by deed; in writing; or evidenced in writing.

. . . .

CAPACITY

The law requires persons entering a contract to have the necessary capacity. All persons of full age have contractual capacity. There are three special cases: corporations; persons of unsound mind including drunkards; and minors.

Corporations

Corporations are classified, according to the manner in which they are created, as being registered, statutory and chartered.

1 Registered Companies

Companies registered under the Companies Act 1985 have capacity to enter into any contract that is within the limits of the "objects" clause of the company's memorandum of association. This is a public document without which a company cannot be registered.

At common law, a company that contracted outside these limits acted ultra vires and any transaction entered into was void; *Ashbury Railway Carriage and Iron Co v Riche*, HL, 1925. However, the Companies Act 1985, s.35 (as amended by the Companies Act 1989), provided that an ultra vires contract may be enforceable against a company by a person dealing with the company in good faith, providing the transaction has been decided upon by the directors.

The ultra vires rule was therefore effectively abolished with regard to innocent third parties dealing with the company in good faith. The Companies Act 2006, s.39(1), now provides that the validity of an act done by a company cannot be called into question on the ground of lack of capacity by anything in the company's constitution.

2 Statutory Corporations

These are corporations created by Act of Parliament. The contractual capacity of such corporations is to be found in the incorporating statute; any contract entered into outside the powers contained in the statute is ultra vires and void.

3 Chartered Corporations

Corporations set up by Royal Charter (e.g. charitable associations and some universities) possess the same contractual capacity as a natural person of full age and capacity.

Persons of Unsound Mind and Drunkards

As a general rule, a contract with a person suffering from mental disability or drunkenness is valid, unless the person is, at the time of the contract, incapable of understanding the nature of the transaction and the other party is aware of this; *Molton v Camroux*, 1849. In such circumstances, the contract is voidable at the mentally impaired or drunken person's option.

Where, however, the other party (of sound mind) is unaware of the other's disability, the contract will be judged by the same standards as if the contract were between two persons of sound minds; *Hart v O'Connor*, PC, 1985. Thus, the transaction would only be set aside if unconscionable (see Chapter 10).

Section 3 of the Sale of Goods Act 1979 provides that persons under such disability will be liable to pay a reasonable sum for necessary goods sold and delivered to them.

Persons may be suffering such a degree of mental disability that their affairs come under the protection of the court under the Mental Capacity Act 2005. Any contracts made by such persons are under the control of the court and contracts made personally are unenforceable against the mental patient.

Minors

Persons below the age of 18 are regarded in law as minors (or infants). Contracts made with minors fall into three categories: contracts valid at common law; contracts voidable at common law; and other contracts.

1 Contracts Valid at Common Law

Contracts for the sale of necessary goods sold and actually delivered to the minor are binding upon him or her. Necessary goods are those suitable to the minor's station in life and his or her actual requirements at the time of delivery; the court will have regard to whether the minor is already adequately supplied with the particular goods.

KEY CASE

NASH V INMAN, CA, 1908

The defendant was a Cambridge undergraduate and whilst under the age of majority purchased clothing from the claimant, a Savile Row tailor, including 11 fancy waistcoats. The evidence was that the defendant was already adequately supplied with clothing suitable to his station in life.

Held: In the circumstances the goods were not necessaries and the claimant's action to recover the cost of the goods failed.

Comment

It should be noted that the minor's obligation is to pay a reasonable price for the goods, not necessarily the contract price.

The minor is likewise bound to pay a reasonable sum for necessary services, although in this case the contract is binding even if only executory; *Roberts v Gray*, CA, 1913.

The minor is also bound by beneficial contracts of service, apprenticeship and analogous contracts. In *Proform Sports Management Ltd v Proactive Sports Management Ltd*, 2006 a football agency agreement between a young player (Wayne Rooney) and a company was held not to be analogous to a contract of service—it did not in any way contribute to his ability earn a living nor was it a contract for necessaries.

---

2 Contracts Voidable at Common Law

Certain contracts are voidable by the minor. These are contracts for the sale or purchase of land; leases; contracts to buy shares; marriage settlements and partnership agreements. Such contracts are enforceable by the minor, and binding upon him or her unless repudiated during minority or within a reasonable time after attaining majority.

3 Other Contracts

At common law other contracts were also said to be "voidable", but in the sense that they were not binding on the minor unless ratified by him or her on attaining majority. However, the Infants Relief Act 1874 rendered loans and contracts for the supply of non-necessary goods entered into by minors "absolutely void". This Act was not without its difficulties and was repealed by the Minors' Contracts Act 1987, s.1 and therefore the common law position referred to above once again applies. The position at common law with regard to the contracts referred to in 1. and 2. (above) also remains unchanged.

Section 2 of the 1987 Act overrules *Coutts v Browne-Lecky*, 1947 and renders guarantees made by adults of loans advanced to minors enforceable against the adult guarantor. Section 3 provides a restitutionary remedy for an adult who has entered into an enforceable contract with a minor. Before the Act, non-necessary goods acquired by the minor were generally irrecoverable by the adult party, even where the minor had lied about his or her age: *Leslie v Shiell*, CA, 1914. However, the court may now, if just and equitable, require the minor to transfer to the adult any property acquired by the minor under the contract or any property representing it.

FORMALITIES

> **CHECKPOINT**
>
> As a general rule, the law does not require any formalities (i.e. writing) to render a contract valid and enforceable. Nevertheless, certain contracts are required to be by deed, others to be in writing and one type of contract is required to be evidenced in writing.

Contracts Which Must Be by Deed

A lease for more than three years must be made by deed, and if not by deed, is void for the purpose of creating a legal estate. Gratuitous promises (i.e. without consideration) may be rendered enforceable by a deed.

Contracts Which Must Be in Writing

A contract may be required to be made in a written form by the provisions of a statute. For example, the Consumer Credit Act 1974 (as amended by the Consumer Credit Act 2006) requires consumer credit agreements to be made in a certain form. An agreement which is not properly executed in accordance with the Act can only be enforced against the debtor on an order of the court.

Until 1989, contracts for the sale or other disposition of an interest in land were required to be evidenced in writing by virtue of s.40 of the Law of Property Act 1925, although the requirement goes back to the Statute of

Frauds 1677. Even where there was insufficient written evidence the contract might nevertheless be enforceable under the equitable doctrine of part-performance.

LEGISLATION HIGHLIGHTER

The **Law Reform (Miscellaneous Provisions) Act 1989,** which came into force on September 27, 1989, repealed s.40 of the **Law of Property Act 1925** and set out new rules governing formalities which are required for all contracts for the sale or other disposition of an interest in land. The equitable doctrine of part-performance disappeared.

The basic requirement of the regime is that all contracts relating to interests in land must be written and signed by the parties. Section 2 provides:

(1) A contract for the sale or other disposition of an interest in land can only be made in writing and only by incorporating all the terms which the parties have expressly agreed in one document or, where contracts are exchanged, in each.

(2) The terms may be incorporated in a document either by being set out in it or by reference to some other document.

(3) The document incorporating the terms, or, where contracts are exchanged, one of the documents incorporating them (but not necessarily the same one) must be signed by, or on behalf of, each party to the contract.

In *Spiro v Glencrown Properties Ltd*, 1991 it was held that the requirements of s.2 applied to the grant of an option for the sale of land.

Excluded from the rules are:

(1) contracts for the grant of short leases;

(2) contracts regulated under the Financial Services Act 1986;

(3) contracts made in the course of a public auction.

Contracts Which Must Be Evidenced in Writing

Contracts of guarantee are required by statute to be "evidenced in writing". The requirement of written evidence means that there must be some written note or memorandum of the transaction in existence before the contract is sought to be enforced. It must be signed by the party to be made liable or by some other person lawfully authorised by him. For the purpose of the latter the contract may be enforceable where the person authorised signs only in an agency capacity; *The Maria D*, HL, 1991.

Section 4 of the Statute of Frauds 1677 provides that a "promise to answer for the debt, default or miscarriage of another person" must be evidenced in writing. The section refers to a promise by one party to answer for the contractual (or tortious) liability of another. For example, suppose A (the principal debtor) owes money to B (the creditor). If a third party, C, promises to pay the debt to B if A fails to pay, C acts as guarantor of A's liability. The contract is one of guarantee and therefore caught by s.4. If, however, the third party C makes his promise to the principal debtor A, the transaction will not be a contract of guarantee; *Eastwood v Kenyon*, 1840.

A contract of guarantee must be distinguished from a contract of indemnity, which is not caught by s.4. In a contract of indemnity, C takes over the liability of A and A is discharged. Thus, in *Goodman v Chase*, 1818, C obtained the debtor A's release from custody by orally promising the sheriff, B, that he, C, would pay A's debt. C having assumed primary liability, it was held that the transaction was an (enforceable) indemnity.

Where there has never been a debt between A and B, C's promise cannot be in the nature of a guarantee; *Lakeman v Mounstephen*, HL, 1874.

KEY CASE

Actionstrength Ltd v International Glass Engineering (Inglen) Spa, HL, 2003

A agreed with Inglen that A would supply labour to enable Inglen to build a factory for S. Inglen fell into arrears with payment to A and A threatened to withdraw its labour. Accordingly S induced A not to do this by orally promising A that, if Inglen did not pay A, S would do so (a contract of guarantee). Ultimately A, unable to obtain payment from Inglen, proceeded against S, who pleaded the absence of a memorandum as required by s.4. A argued that S was estopped from relying on the Statute as A had relied on the promise of S to its detriment.

Held: A's action failed. To permit an estoppel to avoid the application of the Statute to an oral contract of guarantee would be inconsistent with the terms of the Statute.

Comment

The House of Lords considered that if S were held to be estopped in this case, it was hard to see why any oral guarantee where credit was extended to a debtor on the strength of a guarantee would not be similarly estopped. The result would be to circumvent a provision that Parliament had deliberately chosen to retain.

Exceptional Cases

A contract of guarantee only comes within s.4 if it stands on its own. The following exceptions (i.e. cases where there is no requirement of written evidence) are established.

1. Guarantee forms part of a larger transaction. In *Sutton v Grey*, 1894, Grey agreed to introduce clients to a firm of stockbrokers. It was orally agreed that Grey should have half the commission earned as a result of the introductions and that he would be liable for half of any loss caused by the default of clients. It was held that although the latter promise was a guarantee, it did not come within s.4 as it formed part of a larger transaction.

2. Guarantee given to release property from liability. In *Fitzgerald v Dressler*, 1859, B sold linseed to A, who resold at a higher price to C. B remained in possession of the goods under a lien until he received payment from A. In order to obtain immediate possession of the goods, C undertook to guarantee A's debt to B. It was held that the transaction was outside s.4.

In order to fall within this exception, the guarantor must be the substantial owner of the property in respect of which the guarantee is given. In *Harburg India Rubber Comb Co v Martin*, CA, 1902, a promise given by a shareholder to guarantee the company's debts did not fall within the exception.

CONSUMER PROTECTION (DISTANCE SELLING) REGULATIONS 2000

Another example of legislation prescribing contractual formalities is the Distance Selling Regulations. The regulations apply to "distance contracts", that is:

> "any contract concerning goods or services concluded between a seller and consumer under an organised distance sales or service provision scheme run by the supplier who, for the purposes of the contract, makes exclusive use of one or more means of distance communication up to and including the moment when the contract is concluded" (reg.3(1)).

Schedule 1 of the regulations contains a list of methods of distance communication to which the regulations apply, including:

> letter; press advertising with order forms; catalogue; telephone; radio; videophone; email; fax; internet; and teleshopping.

LIVERPOOL JOHN MOORES UNIVERSITY
LEARNING SERVICES

The regulations require certain information to be given to the consumer prior to the conclusion of the contract, including:

> the identity of the supplier; a description of the goods and services; the price; delivery costs; and the existence of a right of cancellation (reg.7(1)).

The supplier must ensure that this information is given in a form appropriate to the form of distance communication used (reg.7(2)).

Regulation 8 requires the supplier to confirm in writing, or another durable medium (e.g. email), the information already given and also some additional information, including information on the right to cancel the contract. There is a "cooling-off period" (i.e. right to cancel) of seven working days from the day after the date of the contract in the case of services, or from the day after the date of delivery of the goods. Where the supplier fails to comply with the information requirement at all, the cooling-off period is extended to three months (regs 10–12).

Under reg.5, certain contracts are excluded from the regulations, including: sales of land and construction agreements (other than rental agreements); financial services; contracts concluded by automated machines, via public pay phones and at auction.

REVISION CHECKLIST

You should now know and understand:

☐ those special cases where the contractual capacity of parties is limited;

☐ the types of contracts where form is required and the nature of the formalities in each case.

Figure 9: Formalities

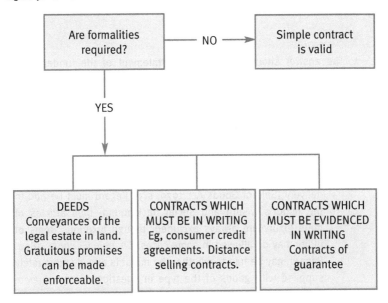

```
┌─────────────────┐                    ┌─────────────────┐
│ Are formalities │ ──── NO ────────▶  │ Simple contract │
│   required?     │                    │    is valid     │
└─────────────────┘                    └─────────────────┘
         │
        YES
         │
         ▼
```

DEEDS Conveyances of the legal estate in land. Gratuitous promises can be made enforceable.	CONTRACTS WHICH MUST BE IN WRITING Eg, consumer credit agreements. Distance selling contracts.	CONTRACTS WHICH MUST BE EVIDENCED IN WRITING Contracts of guarantee

QUESTION AND ANSWER

THE QUESTION

"All contracts entered into by minors are unenforceable against them."

Discuss the validity of the above statement and consider whether it represents a fully correct statement of the law regarding the contractual capacity of minors.

ADVICE AND THE ANSWER

General guidance

Although the contractual capacity of minors is a topic which has diminished in significance since the lowering of the age of majority to 18 in 1969, cases can still arise. To tackle a question on this topic effectively, you will need to have some understanding of the law as it was prior to the passing of the Minors' Contracts Act 1987 as well as the established exceptions to the principle in the above quotation. The law regarding minors' contracts is more complex than one might expect. The plan below gives an indication of the structure and scope of an answer to the question.

Answer plan

1 The answer should begin with a statement of the fundamental position, i.e. that contracts are not binding on minors—the assumption is that they are in need of protection from adults. There are three exceptional contracts, below:

2 (a) Contracts for necessaries—where necessary goods are sold and delivered to a minor, he must pay a reasonable price for them. "Necessaries" means goods suitable to the condition in life of the minor and to his actual requirements at the time of sale and delivery (Sale of Goods Act 1979, s.3). Regard must be had to the minor's wealth and social background—thus articles of mere luxury are always excluded, though luxurious items of utility may be allowed in some cases; *Chapple v Cooper*, 1844. Regard may be had to whether the minor is already adequately supplied with goods of the type in question; *Nash v Inman*, 1908. The minor is only liable to pay a reasonable sum on an executed contract, although in *Roberts v Gray*, CA, 1913, a partially executed contract for a necessary service (an apprenticeship to a professional billiards player) was upheld.

(b) Beneficial contracts of service—contracts entered into by minors for education, apprenticeship or employment will be upheld providing the contract is, on the whole, for the minor's benefit. It may be beneficial even though it contains some onerous provisions; *Clements v London & North Western Railway Co*, 1894. Cf. *De Francesco v Barnum*, 1890, where the terms of a young stage dancer's apprenticeship contract were too extreme to be enforceable. The courts may uphold contracts that are analogous to contracts of service; *Chaplin v Leslie Frewin (Publishers) Ltd*, CA, 1966 (contract for a minor to write a book). Trading contracts, however, will never be binding on minors; *Cowern v Nield*, 1912.

(c) Voidable contracts—"voidable" contracts are binding on both parties unless repudiated by the minor either during minority or within a reasonable time after attaining majority. These are transactions where the minor acquires an interest in the subject-matter involving continuing or recurring obligations. Relevant contracts include: marriage settlements; partnership agreements; liabilities in relation to shareholding; and contracts in relation to an interest in land.

Where a minor repudiates a void contract, the law is unclear as to whether the minor will be liable for obligations that have already arisen at the date of the contract. Whether the minor can recover moneys paid under the contract before repudiation depends on there being a total failure of consideration: *cf. Corpe v Overton*, 1833, and *Steinberg v Scala (Leeds) Ltd*, 1923.

3 Other contracts. At common law, contracts made by minors which do not fall into one of the above categories are not binding on the minor. Thus, to this extent, the proposition stated in the question above is correct. The minor may ratify such a contract on attaining majority, a right restored to the minor by the Minors' Contracts Act 1987 repealing s.2 of the Infants Relief Act 1874.

4 A restitutionary remedy was introduced by s.3 of the Act of 1987, as an alternative to restitution in equity. Thus where a contract is unenforceable against the minor, the court may, if it is just and equitable to do so, require the minor to restore any property acquired under the contract to the adult party. The concept of "property" under the Act may extend to money.

5 Under the Infants Relief Act 1874, loans to minors (and probably guarantees of such loans) were "absolutely void". The Act of 1874 has been repealed—in its place the Minors' Contracts Act 1987, s.2, provides that such a guarantee shall not be unenforceable merely on the ground of the minority of the principal debtor.

Terms of the Contract

INTRODUCTION

In this chapter we are concerned with the contents of the contract itself. The following issues are considered:

1 The need for certainty of terms
2 The distinction between representations and terms
3 The classification of contractual terms
4 The circumstances in which terms will be implied into a contract

Contracts consist of various statements, promises, stipulations, etc., grouped together under the word "terms". The terms may be express or implied. It is the terms of the contract which determine the extent of each party's rights and duties and the remedies available if the terms are broken are determined by the comparative importance of the terms.

CERTAINTY OF TERMS

A contract may be void if the terms are not reasonably certain. In *Scammell v Ouston*, HL, 1941, the House of Lords held an arrangement to acquire a van "on hire-purchase terms" too vague to be an enforceable contract.

In commercial transactions, the court may be prepared to enforce an ostensibly vague agreement by reference to trade custom or any previous dealings between the parties; *Hillas Co Ltd v Arcos Ltd*, HL, 1932. Where a contract for the sale of goods does not fix a price, the Sale of Goods Act 1979 s.8 provides that a reasonable price must be paid.

It is possible that the parties themselves may provide the machinery for resolving an apparently uncertain term, such as where the price of land is to be fixed by valuers appointed by the parties; *Sudbrook Trading Estate Ltd v Eggleton*, HL, 1982. The *Sudbrook* case was distinguished in *Gillatt v Sky Television Ltd*, CA, 2000. In that case the contract provided that the value of shares was to be determined by an independent chartered accountant. The Court of Appeal held that the appointment of an accountant was not merely a mechanism or permissive procedure, but an essential condition precedent to the existence of any entitlement under the contract.

Another possibility is that the contract provides machinery for resolving the uncertainty in the form of an appropriately drafted arbitration clause. In *Foley v Classique Coaches Ltd*, CA, 1934, the claimant owned a petrol station and the land adjacent. The defendants operated a coach company and the claimants entered into an agreement to sell them the adjoining land, on condition that they entered into an agreement to buy petrol "at a price to be agreed by the parties". There was a further clause which stated that any dispute arising out of the agreement should be submitted to arbitration. The agreement was performed for three years before a dispute arose. It was held that there was a binding contract; not only was there an arbitration clause but there had been performance under the contract. The court implied a term that the petrol should be supplied at a reasonable price.

Performance is a highly significant factor in influencing a court to uphold a contract of which the terms are uncertain; *RTS Flexible Systems Ltd v Molkerei Alois Muller GmbH*, SC, 2010. But performance will not inevitably mean that the contract is enforceable, if essential terms are yet to be agreed; *British Steel Corporation v Cleveland Bridge Engineering Co Ltd*, 1984.

If an uncertain term is actually meaningless, then exceptionally the court may be prepared to sever the provision if it is clearly superfluous. In *Nicolene Ltd v Simmonds*, CA, 1953, a contract for the sale of goods contained the words, "I assume ... that the usual conditions of acceptance apply." As there were no usual conditions of acceptance, the Court of Appeal held the words were meaningless and could be ignored.

It seems that where the parties intend to create a contractual obligation, the court will try to give it legal effect. The contract will only be void for uncertainty "if it is legally or practically impossible to give the agreement ... any sensible content"; *Durham Tees Valley Airport Ltd v Bmibaby Ltd*, CA, 2010.

THE PAROL EVIDENCE RULE

There is a general rule, the "parol evidence rule", that where a contract is embodied in a written document, then extrinsic (parol) evidence is not admissible to add to, vary, subtract from or contradict the terms of the written document. Extrinsic evidence is not confined to oral statements but can extend to written matter such as draft contracts and correspondence. The inconvenience and injustice of the rule is obvious and the courts have evaded it by creating a number of exceptions. The Law Commission (1976) recommended that the rule be abolished.

The main exceptions to the parol evidence rule are as follows:

(1) Custom. Evidence of the customs of a locality or trade usage can be admitted to add to, but not contradict, a written agreement; *Palgrave Brown and Son Ltd v SS. Turid*, HL, 1922.

(2) Operation of the contract. Extrinsic evidence is permissible to show that the contract has not yet come into operation or has ceased to operate. In *Pym v Campbell*, 1856, there was a written agreement for the sale of a share in a patent but the parties orally agreed that the agreement was not to operate until a third party approved the invention. Evidence of the oral agreement was admitted.

(3) Validity. Extrinsic evidence is admissible to show that the contract is invalid for mistake, misrepresentation, incapacity or want of consideration.

(4) Evidence as to supplementary terms. There is a presumption that where the contract is reduced to writing, the writing is intended to include all the terms of the contract. This presumption may be rebutted by showing that the contract is partly written and partly oral; *Walker Property Investments Ltd v Walker*, CA, 1947.

(5) Rectification. The equitable remedy of rectification is an exception to the parol evidence rule (see Chapter 9).

(6) Collateral contract. Extrinsic evidence of a collateral contract is admissible; *City of Westminster Properties Ltd v Mudd*, 1959. Collateral contracts are discussed below, under "Representations and Terms".

Figure 10: Certainty of Terms

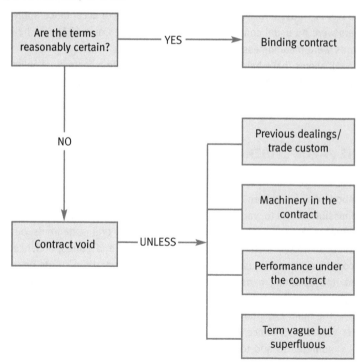

REPRESENTATIONS AND TERMS

Statements made by the parties in the course of negotiations leading up to the formation of the contract are classified by the court as either representations or terms. A representation is a statement which induces the contract but does not form part of it, whereas a term is a promise or undertaking that is part of the contract itself. If a representation proves false, the remedy will lie in an action for misrepresentation (see Chapter 8), whereas if a term is broken the remedy will lie in an action for breach of contract (see below). In some cases, a misrepresentation later becomes incorporated into the contract as a term. In such a case the injured party will have two causes of action: one for misrepresentation and the other for breach.

Whether a statement is a representation or a term is primarily a question of intention. If the parties have indicated that a statement is to be regarded as a term, the court will implement their intention. In other cases, the following guidelines may be applied:

Manner and Timing of Statement

A statement is not likely to be a term if the person making the statement asks the other party to check or verify it, as where the seller of a boat stated that it was sound but asked the buyer to have it surveyed; *Ecay v Godfrey*, 1947. If the statement is made with the intention of preventing the other from finding a defect, and succeeds in this, the court may consider it to be a term. Thus, in *Schawel v Reade*, HL, 1913, the vendor of a horse said to the buyer, "You need not look for anything, the horse is perfectly sound," and the House of Lords held that the statement was a term. Where there is a distinct interval of time between the making of the statement and the conclusion of the contract, this may indicate that the parties do not intend the statement to be a term; *Routledge v McKay*, CA, 1954. In the case of *Inntrepreneur Pub Co v East Crown Ltd*, 2000, Lightman J said that the longer the interval between the statement and the contract, "the greater the presumption must be that the parties did not intend the statement to have contractual effect".

Importance of Statement

A statement is likely to be a term if it is such that the injured party would not have entered into the contract had it not been made. In *Bannerman v White*, 1861, a prospective purchaser of hops asked whether they had been treated with sulphur, adding that if they had, he would not even trouble to ask the price. The seller's (erroneous) statement that sulphur had not been used was held to be a term.

Special Knowledge and Skill

Where one of the parties possesses superior knowledge and skill relating to the subject-matter, the court may conclude that any statement made by such a party is a term.

KEY CASE

DICK BENTLEY PRODUCTIONS LTD V HAROLD SMITH (MOTORS) LTD, CA, 1965

The claimant told the defendant, a car dealer, that he wished to buy a "well-vetted" Bentley car. The defendant showed the claimant a car which, he said, had done only 20,000 miles since being fitted with a new engine. The statement as to mileage was untrue, as the car had done over 100,000 miles since reconditioning. The claimant sought damages for breach of contract.

Held: The statement as to mileage was a term of the contract. The defendant, being a dealer, had special knowledge and skill compared with the defendant.

Comment

The court in this case distinguished the earlier case of *Oscar Chess Ltd v Williams*, CA, 1957 where, on a part-exchange deal, a private car owner falsely (but honestly) stated the age of the car to the dealer. The statement was held to be a representation; the dealer was in at least as strong a position to verify the truth of the statement.

Statement Reduced to Writing

Where the agreement has been reduced to a written document, statements appearing in the written contract will normally be regarded as terms. Subject to the matters discussed above, statements excluded from the written contract are likely to be regarded as representations. Nevertheless, the court will look to the intention of the parties to see whether they intended a contract partly written and partly oral; *J. Evans and Son (Portsmouth) Ltd v Andrea Merzario Ltd*, CA, 1976.

It may be possible to avoid the argument that a contract is partly written and partly oral by the insertion of an "entire agreement" clause in the written contract. Such a clause states that the written document is intended and agreed to contain the entirety of the contract, each party acknowledging that they have not relied on any representation or statement not contained in the written document.

An entire agreement clause will require careful drafting in order to exclude liability for misrepresentation—it must be completely unambiguous; *Axa Sun Life Services Plc v Campbell Martin Ltd*, CA, 2011.

COLLATERAL CONTRACTS

Where a contract is entered into on the faith of a statement made by one of the parties, there may be a secondary or "collateral" contract based upon the statement.

In *De Lassalle v Guildford*, CA, 1901, the defendant was negotiating the lease of a house to the claimant, who refused to complete unless the defendant orally assured him that the drains were in order. The defendant gave such an assurance, but no term to that effect was inserted into the lease document. The drains were not in order and the claimant sued for damages not upon the lease (which did not refer to the drains), but on a collateral contract based on the defendant's oral assurance. The consideration to enforce this promise as a separate contract was the claimant's execution of the lease, i.e. his entering into the main contract.

The following points should be noted in connection with collateral contracts:

(1) Although the collateral contract is essentially a judicial device, the court will not find such a contract unless all the elements of a separate valid contract are present; *Heilbut, Symons Co v Buckleton*, HL, 1913.

(2) A collateral contract may be valid even though it conflicts with a term in the main contract. In *City of Westminster Properties Ltd v Mudd*, 1959, a lease contained a covenant that the premises should only be used for business. The tenant residing there was only induced to sign the lease by an oral assurance by the landlord that he could continue to do so. It was held that the oral assurance formed the basis of a collateral contract which could be raised as a defence in an action for breach of covenant by the landlord.

(3) The collateral contract device proved useful in circumventing the rule that damages were not available for non-fraudulent misrepresentation. Since damages are now available for such misrepresentation (see Chapter 8), the device has lost some of its significance. It may, however, be used to sidestep the parol evidence rule and has been used in certain other contexts, e.g. to avoid the effects of an illegal contract (see Chapter 11); and to avoid the privity rule (see chapter 12). The decision in *Record v Bell*, 1991 shows that the collateral contract device can be relied upon in certain circumstances to get around s.2 of the Law of Property (Miscellaneous Provisions) Act 1989.

(4) In the *Inntrepreneur* case (see above) it was held (following *Deepak Fertilisers and Petrochemical Corp v Davy McKee (London) Ltd*, 1999) that an entire agreement clause in an agreement for a lease of a public house precluded the tenant setting up a collateral contract as a defence to an action for breach of contract.

Figure 11: Pre-contractual Statements

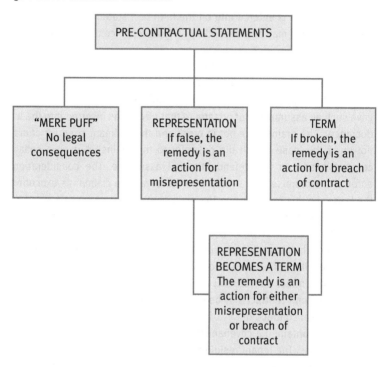

CONDITIONS, WARRANTIES AND INNOMINATE TERMS

CHECKPOINT

Not all the terms of the contract are of equal importance and the law classifies them according to their importance. The normal classification is to divide them into "conditions", "warranties" and "innominate" terms. These terms are discussed below.

Condition

The word "condition" may be used to denote a condition precedent or condition subsequent (i.e. events upon which the existence of the contract depends; see *Pym v Campbell*, 1856 and *Head v Tattersall*, 1871) but it is most commonly used to describe an important term of the contract. The breach of a condition will entitle the injured party to treat himself as discharged from the contract as well as giving him the right to sue for damages.

Where a term is classified as a condition, the injured party will have a right to repudiate the contract even where the effects of the breach are trivial, or where they have an ulterior motive for termination, such as an adverse change in market conditions.

Warranty

The word "warranty" is commonly used to denote a contractual term of lesser importance, the breach of which gives the injured party the right to claim damages only and not to treat himself as discharged from the contract.

Whether a term is a condition or a warranty depends on the intention of the parties. An illustration of the distinction is to be found by contrasting *Poussard v Spiers*, 1876 (condition) and *Bettini v Gye*, 1876 (warranty). In *Poussard*, an opera singer's obligation to sing on the first night of a three-month series of concerts was held to be a condition; in *Bettini*, the singer's obligation to attend all the rehearsals was held to be a warranty.

The fact that the parties have described a term in the contract as a "condition" may not be conclusive.

KEY CASE

L. Schuler A.G. v Wickman Machine Tool Sales Ltd, HL, 1974
The contract stated that it was "a condition of this agreement" that the defendants should make 1,400 visits to six named car companies over a four-and-a-half-year period. The defendants failed to carry out all of the visits. The claimants argued that since the term was described as a "condition", any breach (e.g. the failure to make one visit) would justify termination.

Held: It was not the case that that the failure to make one visit should entitle the other party to terminate the contract. The parties could not have intended the term to operate as a condition in circumstances where it produced such an unreasonable result.

Comment
Although not concerned with the meaning of "condition", a similar approach was followed in *Rice v Great Yarmouth Borough Council*, CA,

2000, where there was a clause in a long term leisure management agreement that "if the contractor committed a breach of any of its obligations under the contract ... the council ... may terminate [the contract]". The court held that the clause could not have been intended by the parties to apply to minor breaches, but only those giving rise to a right to terminate the contract.

Innominate Term

The above definitions of conditions and warranties derive from the Sale of Goods Act 1893 (now enacted in the Sale of Goods Act 1979) but came to be applied by the courts to other types of contract apart from the sale of goods. The classification is based upon an examination of the contract itself to ascertain whether the parties intended a particular term to be a condition or a warranty. It has the merit of certainty in that the consequences of a breach (termination or damages) may be predicted in advance.

More recently the courts have looked at the effect of a breach on the injured party to ascertain whether a condition or a warranty has been broken. A term will be classed as "innominate" where it is only when the effects of its breach are considered that its true nature is revealed. The merit of this approach is flexibility. The following key case is the leading case on the innominate approach.

KEY CASE

HONG KONG FIR SHIPPING CO LTD V KAWASAKI KISEN KAISHA LTD, CA, 1962

The defendants chartered a ship from the claimants for a period of two years. The engines were antiquated and the staff incompetent with the result that 20 weeks were lost. The defendants repudiated the charter, alleging breach of a "condition" to provide a seaworthy ship. The claimants brought an action for wrongful repudiation, arguing that their breach was not such as entitled the defendants to terminate the contract, but only to claim damages.

Held: The court found for the claimants; the question to be asked was whether, looking at the events which had occurred as a result of the breach, the defendants had been deprived of the whole of the benefit to which they were entitled under the contract. The court answered the question in the negative; the breach was not such as justified termination.

Comment

Despite the judicial reluctance to classify terms as conditions or

> warranties, the courts are prepared to do so if the circumstances require it. In *The Mihalis Angelos*, CA, 1971, it was held that a clause in a charter-party that a ship would be ready to load on a certain date was a condition, and in *Bunge Corp v Tradax S.A.*, HL, 1981, the court arrived at a similar decision concerning the time-table in a contract of sale.

In *The Hansa Nord*, CA, 1975 the court said that it was wrong to assume, even in a contract governed by the Sale of Goods Act, that a term was either a condition or a warranty. It was possible to have an "intermediate" (innominate) term, where the remedy for breach (termination or damages) would depend upon the nature of the breach.

IMPLIED TERMS

There are three ways in which terms which have not been expressed may be implied into the contract: by the court, by custom and by statute.

1 Terms implied by the court
Where a term is not expressly stated, but is one which the parties, in the view of the court, must have intended to include as necessary in order to make the contract workable, the term may be implied into the contract. Such terms are classified as "Terms Implied in Fact". In 2009 the Privy Council in the *Belize Telecom* case indicated that the various traditional formulations of the test for implying terms in fact should be condensed into a single proposition. Before considering this key case, the pre-existing formulations adopted by the courts must be considered.

Under one of the traditional tests for implying such a term, the term to be implied must be: "something so obvious that it goes without saying; so that, if while the parties were making their bargain, an officious bystander were to suggest some express provision for it in the agreement, they would testily suppress him with a common: 'Oh, of course!' "— *Shirlaw v Southern Foundries Ltd*, CA, 1939.

A test of necessity is to be seen in *The Moorcock*, CA, 1889 where the defendants, who were wharf-owners, agreed to allow the plaintiffs to unload a vessel. The vessel grounded at low tide and was damaged. Despite the absence of an express term, the defendants were held liable for breach of an implied term to take reasonable care that the berth was safe. The implied term was necessary in order to give the contract business efficacy.

A term cannot be implied where one of the parties has no knowledge of the matter to be implied; *Spring v National Amalgamated Stevedores and Dockers Society*, 1956. It is also the case that there can be no implication of a term to which one party would clearly have not agreed; *National Bank of Greece S.A. v Pinios Shipping Co*, CA, 1989. It is irrelevant that the term which is sought to be implied would make the contract more reasonable; *Liverpool CC v Irwin*, HL, 1977.

KEY CASE

ATTORNEY-GENERAL OF BELIZE V BELIZE TELECOM, PC, 2009
In this case, Lord Hoffmann considered that the implication of a term was an exercise in the construction of the contract as a whole. In every case of a suggested implied term, the question for the court is whether such a provision would spell out expressly what the contract, read against the relevant background, would reasonably be understood to mean. The question can be formulated using the traditional tests (if the court finds it helpful) but these are not different or additional tests. Lord Hoffmann said: "There is only one question: is that what the instrument, read as a whole against the relevant background, would reasonably be understood to mean?"

Comment
Thus the various formulations of the test for implying terms in fact (including the "officious bystander" test and the "necessity" test) have been condensed into a single proposition. Post-*Belize Telecom*, some cases, whilst acknowledging Lord Hoffmann's approach, have continued to make express reference to the test of necessity; e.g. *Mediterranean Salvage and Towage Ltd v Seamar Trading and Commerce Inc*, CA, 2009. In *SNCB Holding v UBS AG*, 2012, the court referred to the traditional tests but considered that Lord Hoffmann's notion that the "proposed implied term must spell out what the contract actually means" was sufficient to encompass these tests.

A term may also be implied by the court, not according to the parties' intentions but as a matter of law ("Terms Implied in Law"). Many of these implied terms are well-established in the law concerning particular types of contract, such as master and servant; and landlord and tenant. Thus, in *Liverpool CC v Irwin*, the House of Lords held that it was an implied term in a tenancy agreement of a council flat that the landlord should take reasonable care to keep lifts and staircases in a reasonable state of repair. It should be noted that many such terms have been incorporated into statutes, e.g. the Sale of Goods Act 1979; the Supply of Goods and Services Act 1982.

2 Terms implied by custom

Terms may be implied into a contract by adducing evidence of local custom or trade usage with respect to matters upon which the contract is silent; *Hutton v Warren*, 1836. A custom will not be implied if it is contrary to the express terms of the contract; *Les Affreteurs Reunis SA v Walford*, HL, 1919.

3 Terms implied by statute

Certain statutes imply terms into particular types of contract. An example of a statute which implies terms into contracts is the Late Payment of Commercial Debts (Interest) Act 1998. Where it applies, the Act provides for an implied term that any qualifying debt carries interest; however, the Act may be excluded in certain situations.

LEGISLATION HIGHLIGHTER

Of particular importance are the terms implied by the **Sale of Goods Act 1979** into contracts for the sale of goods. In essence, the implied terms are as follows:

1 Title. There is an implied condition that a seller has the right to sell the goods and implied warranties that the goods are free from encumbrances and that the buyer will enjoy quiet possession (s.12).

2 Description. There is an implied condition that the goods will correspond with the description (s.13).

3 Fitness for purpose and satisfactory quality. Where goods are sold in the course of a business, there is an implied condition that the goods shall be reasonably fit for the purpose for which they are required and an implied term that the goods shall be of satisfactory quality (s.14).

4 Sale by sample. In such a sale, there are various implied conditions including a condition that the bulk corresponds with the sample in quality (s.15).

NB. The above provisions do not apply to "consumer contracts" under the **Consumer Rights Act 2014**. Instead, that Act, when it has been brought into force, will insert corresponding terms as between trader and consumer.

There are similar statutory implied terms in contracts of hire-purchase and contracts for the supply of goods. The extent to which such implied terms may be excluded by the parties is considered in Chapter 7.

CONSUMER CONTRACTS

The Consumer Rights Act, Part 1, will introduce a category of "consumer contracts" for goods, digital content and services. The Act consolidates and re-enacts the pre-existing sale and supply of goods law relating to *business to consumer* contracts in one new piece of legislation.

Part 1 applies where there is a contract between a trader and a consumer under which a trader agrees to supply goods, digital content or services—or any combination of these—to a consumer.

"Trader" means a person (including companies) acting for purposes relating to their trade, business, craft or profession. "Business" includes the activities of governmental, local and public authorities.

"Consumer" means an individual (i.e. a natural person) acting for purposes wholly or mainly outside their trade, business, craft or profession.

Part 2, Chapter 2 of the Act covers contracts where a trader agrees to supply goods to a consumer. It includes sales contracts, a contract for the hire of goods, hire-purchase agreements and a contract for the transfer of goods.

Under the Act the consumer's statutory rights under contracts for goods will include certain terms that are to be treated as part of the contract without either party needing to refer to them. These include terms corresponding to the implied terms in sale of goods contracts relating to title, description, fitness for purpose, satisfactory quality and sales by sample (see above).

REVISION CHECKLIST

You should now know and understand:

☐ the circumstances in which contractual terms will be held uncertain;

☐ the significance of the distinction between representations and terms;

☐ the distinction between conditions, warranties and innominate terms;

☐ the circumstances in which terms will be implied into a contract by the court, by custom and by statute.

QUESTION AND ANSWER

THE QUESTION

"There ... are many contractual undertakings of a more complex character which cannot be categorised as being 'conditions' or 'warranties'." (Diplock LJ in *Hong Kong Fir Shipping Co Ltd v Kawasaki Kaisen Kaisha Ltd*, CA, 1962.)

Explain the above statement and consider the advantages and disadvantages, if any, of the approach to the categorisation of contractual terms indicated by Diplock LJ.

ADVICE AND THE ANSWER

General guidance

"Contractual terms" is a key topic in the law of contract. In some respects it is the linchpin around which the whole subject revolves. It follows that issues regarding contractual terms can pop up in any question on the law of contract, but especially in questions on exclusion clauses (see Chapter 7) and remedies (see Chapter 14). Sometimes, however, examiners set questions purely on the topic of contractual terms, and when they do, it is quite possible that it will be an essay-type question. The above question is a typical example; the plan below shows you how a good answer to the question should be structured.

Answer plan

1 The traditional categorisation of contractual terms is to divide them into "conditions" and "warranties"—it is based on the original Sale of Goods Act 1893.

2 A condition is a term that goes to the root of the contract, the breach of which entitles the innocent party to repudiate the contract as well as claiming damages.

3 A warranty is a lesser term ("collateral to the main purpose of the contract") the breach of which is remediable by damages only.

4 Whether a term is a condition or a warranty depends on the intention of the parties judged as at the time of the contract. This is illustrated by the "opera singer" cases—*Poussard v Spiers*, 1876 (condition) and *Bettini v Gye*, 1876, (warranty).

5 If a term is a condition then any breach, however trivial, will justify termination; e.g. *Arcos Ltd v Ronaasen & Son*, 1933. However, it is open to the courts to rule in a particular case that the word "condition" cannot have been meant in its traditional sense; *L. Schuler AG v Wickman Machine Tool Sales Ltd*, HL, 1974.

6 The inflexibility of the condition/warranty dichotomy led to the development of the innominate term—*Hong Kong Fir* case—recognition that some terms of a complex character cannot be categorized as

conditions or warranties. In such cases, the right of termination depends on the consequences of the breach. It is only where the breach deprives the other party of the whole benefit to which they are entitled under the contract that they may repudiate.

7 The "innominate" analysis was applied by the Court of Appeal to a sale of goods contract in *The Hansa Nord*, CA, 1975.

8 However, the courts will apply the traditional approach where commercial certainty requires it; *Bunge Corp v Tradax S.A.*, HL. 1981.

9 The condition/warranty classification has the merit of certainty and predictability—it is of benefit not only to businesses but to consumers. The disadvantage is rigidity—it enables termination for technical breaches where there may be an ulterior motive.

10 The innominate approach has the merit of flexibility (the remedy is tailored to the consequences of the breach), however, there can be uncertainty as there may be some delay before the consequences of the breach are known.

Exclusion Clauses

INTRODUCTION

In this chapter we are concerned with the extent to which liability can be excluded or restricted by an exclusion or limitation clause. The main elements are:

1 The common law rules of incorporation and construction
2 The statutory rules under the Unfair Contract Terms Act 1977 regulating such clauses

A clause may be inserted into a contract which purports to exclude (or financially limit) one party's liability for breach of contract, misrepresentation or negligence.

Historically, the courts have sought by various means to control the use of such clauses and latterly Parliament has intervened, most notably with the Unfair Contract Terms Act 1977 and the Unfair Terms in Consumer Contracts Regulations 1999.

However, the former Act will be amended and the latter regulations revoked by the passing of the Consumer Rights Act 2014. The Act consolidates in one piece of legislation consumer rights relating to contracts for goods, digital content, services and the law relating to unfair terms in consumer contracts. The amendments to the Act of 1977 mean that that Act will in future largely cover business to business contracts; and the requirement of reasonableness in the 1977 Act will no longer apply to consumer contracts. Unfair terms in consumer contracts will be regulated by the provisions in Part 2 of the new Act, outlined at the end of this chapter.

Control by the courts has proceeded on two broad fronts; the defendant may only rely on an exclusion clause if it has been incorporated into the contract, and if, as a matter of construction, it extends to the loss in question. These matters are considered below.

INCORPORATION

Document Signed

If the claimant signs a document purporting to have contractual effect containing an exclusion clause, he is bound by its terms. This is so even if he has not read the document and regardless of whether he understands it or not; *L'Estrange v Graucob*, CA, 1934. However, even a signed document can be rendered wholly or partly ineffective by a misrepresentation as to its effect; in *Curtis v Chemical Cleaning and Dyeing Co Ltd*, CA, 1951, the claimant took a dress to be cleaned. She was induced to sign a document which she was told excluded the defendant's liability for damage to sequins. In fact, the document excluded liability for any damage. The dress was returned stained and it was held that the defendants were not protected by the clause which would only protect them in the event of damage to sequins.

The Requirement of Notice

CHECKPOINT

The requirement of notice means that where the document is unsigned but merely delivered to the other party, then reasonable and sufficient notice of the existence of the exclusion clause must be given.

For the above requirement to be satisfied,
(i) the clause must be contained in a contractual document, i.e. one which the reasonable person would assume to contain contractual terms, and not in a document which merely acknowledges payment, such as a voucher or receipt (*Chapelton v Barry Urban DC*, 1940); and
(ii) the existence of the exclusion clause must be brought to the notice of the other party before or at the time the contract is entered into.

KEY CASE

OLLEY V MARLBOROUGH COURT, CA 1949
The claimant arrived at a hotel and paid for a room at reception; she then proceeded to the room where there was displayed a notice excluding liability for goods lost or stolen. The claimant's jewellery was subsequently stolen from the room. The claimant sued the defendant hotel who sought to rely on the exclusion clause.

Held: The clause was not incorporated—the notice came too late to affect the claimant's rights.

Comment

The defendants might have succeeded if had they displayed a prominent sign containing the clause at the reception desk, or if they had
required the claimant to sign a document in which the term was
included. But she could not be bound by a notice that she had had no
opportunity of seeing at the time of entering the contract.

Where the document is issued by an automatic machine, the Court of Appeal
has taken a strict view. In *Thornton v Shoe Lane Parking Ltd*, CA, 1971, Lord
Denning M.R. decided that conditions on a ticket issued by an automatic car
park barrier came too late; the contract had been concluded a moment
before, at the point when the claimant had placed his vehicle on the spot
which activated the barrier.

It should be noted that reasonable, not actual, notice is required. What
is reasonable is a question of fact depending on all the circumstances and
the situation of the parties; it may depend on the category or class of persons
to which the claimant belongs. In *Thompson v L.M.S. Railway Co*, 1930, an
illiterate railway passenger was held bound by a clause since sufficient
notice had been given to the ordinary railway traveller. In a long line of so-
called "ticket cases", the courts repeatedly held that attention should be
drawn to the existence of excluding terms by clear words on the front of any
document delivered to the claimant, e.g. "for conditions, see back".

It seems that the degree of notice required may increase according to
the gravity or unusualness of the clause in question; *Thornton v Shoe Lane
Parking Ltd*, CA, 1971. It is clear from *Interfoto Picture Library Ltd v Stiletto
Visual Programmes Ltd*, CA, 1988 that this requirement applies to unusual
contract terms generally and not merely to exclusion clauses.

Previous Dealings

Even where there has been insufficient notice, an exclusion clause may
nevertheless be incorporated where there has been a previous course of
dealing between the parties on the same terms; *J. Spurling Ltd v Bradshaw*,
CA, 1956. Thus, the claimant in *Olley v Marlborough Court* (above) might well
have been bound by the clause if she had stayed at the hotel many times
before. The previous course of dealing must have been regular and consistent
(*McCutcheon v David MacBrayne Ltd*, HL, 1964) and it seems that knowledge
of the existence of the clause on the part of the claimant (as opposed to its
content) will suffice in order to bind the claimant by a previous course of
dealing; *Hardwick Game Farm Ltd v Suffolk Agricultural Producer Association*,
HL, 1969. As against a consumer, a considerable number of past transactions
may be required; *Hollier v Rambler Motors (AMC) Ltd*, CA, 1972.

EXCLUSION CLAUSES

A course of dealing was established in *Petrotrade Inc v Texaco Ltd*, CA, 2000. The parties had orally agreed the sale of a cargo and later the claimant sent a telex to the defendant confirming the contract and setting out some additional terms and conditions. The claimant contended that these terms were incorporated on the basis of five previous transactions in the previous 12 months on the same terms. The Court of Appeal held that the terms were indeed incorporated.

Figure 12: Incorporation of a Clause

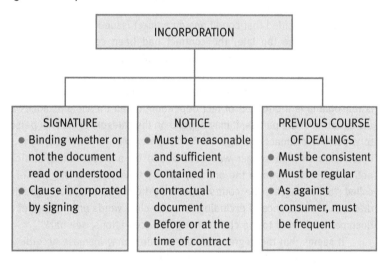

CONSTRUCTION

Once it is established that an exclusion clause is incorporated, the whole contract will be construed (i.e. interpreted) to see whether the clause covers the breach that has occurred. The basic approach is that liability can only be excluded by clear words. The rules of construction, however, should not be applied as strictly to limitation clauses as to exclusion clauses; *Ailsa Craig Fishing Co Ltd v Malvern Fishing Co Ltd*, HL, 1983. The main rules of construction are as follows:

Contra Proferentem Rule

Under this rule, any ambiguity in the wording of an exclusion clause will be construed as narrowly as possible against the party purporting to rely on the clause. Thus, in *Houghton v Trafalgar Insurance Co*, CA, 1954, a car insurance policy excluded the insurer's liability where an excessive "load" was being carried. It was held that the clause did not extend to the situation where a car was carrying an excess of passengers, the word "load" being narrowly construed as referring to goods, not people.

Where it is sought to exclude liability for negligence, particularly clear words are required; *Smith v South Wales Switchgear Ltd*, HL, 1978. The principles are as follows:

(1) If the clause expressly refers to negligence, or uses some synonym for negligence, it will be effective.

(2) In the absence of such express reference, if the words are wide enough to cover negligence the clause may nevertheless be effective, unless there is some liability other than negligence to which the words would apply.

KEY CASE

WHITE V JOHN WARWICK CO LTD, CA, 1953
The claimant was injured riding a cycle hired from the defendants, under a clause stating that "nothing in this agreement shall render the owners liable for personal injury". In supplying the defective cycle, the defendants could have been held liable for both breach of contract and negligence.

Held: The clause was ambiguous and the court construed it to refer to the defendants' contractual liability and so the defendants were not protected if they were found to be negligent.

Comment
By way of contrast, in *Alderslade v Hendon Laundry Ltd*, CA, 1945, the claimant sent articles for laundering which were then lost. The court held that a limitation clause referring to "lost or damaged" articles must apply to negligence since if it did not apply to negligence, it would be redundant (the launderers' only liability in relation to the safe custody of the articles was in negligence).

The above rules are rules of construction only and will not be applied rigidly to defeat the intentions of the parties; *Lictor Anstalt v Mir Steel UK Ltd*, CA, 2012. For example, in *Lamport and Holt Lines Ltd v Coubro and Scrutton Ltd*, CA, 1982, during a refit of the claimant's ship, a derrick collapsed through the defendants' negligence. An exclusion clause referring to damage arising from "any act or omission" was held to be sufficiently wide to embrace negligence, despite the absence of any express reference to, or synonym for, negligence.

It should be noted that construction must also have regard to the principles laid down in *Investors Compensation Scheme Ltd v West Bromwich Building Society*, HL, 1998 and *Chartbrook Ltd v Persimmon Homes Ltd*, HL, 2009, where the court may take into consideration admissible background and the commercial context.

It seems that where contractual words have two possible constructions, the court should strive to prefer the construction that is consistent with commercial commonsense; *Rainy Sky SA v Kookmin Bank*, SC, 2011.

Fundamental Breach

In the 1950s and 1960s, the courts, building on earlier decisions, developed a doctrine that, as a rule of law, an exclusion clause could not protect a party from liability for a serious, i.e. fundamental, breach of contract, even where, on its true construction, the wording of the clause covered the breach which had occurred. The so-called "doctrine of fundamental breach" was rejected by the House of Lords in *Suisse Atlantique Societé d'Armement Maritime S.A. v N.V. Rotterdamsche Kolen Centrale*, HL, 1967 who stated, obiter, that there was no rule of substantive law that an exclusion clause could not cover a fundamental breach; it was a question of construction whether the clause in fact covered the breach in question.

The Court of Appeal effectively revived the rule of law doctrine in *Harbutt's Plasticine Ltd v Wayne Tank and Pump Co Ltd*, CA, 1970 and subsequent cases, albeit in a modified form. In 1980, Harbutt and the cases which followed it were overruled by the House of Lords in *Photo Production Ltd v Securicor Transport Ltd*, HL, 1980, which reaffirmed *Suisse Atlantique*.

In *Photo Production*, the claimants employed the defendants to protect their factory by a visiting patrol. A clause provided that "under no circumstances shall the (defendant) company be responsible for any injurious act or default by any employee of the company". One night, one of the defendants' guards lit a small fire inside the factory which got out of control and completely destroyed the claimant's premises, with loss amounting to £615,000. The House of Lords held that though the defendants were in breach, they were permitted to rely on the clause as it clearly and unambiguously covered the breach in question.

Although the Unfair Contract Terms Act 1977 did not apply to the case (the facts occurred before the Act came into force), the decision is clearly also based on the reasonableness of the clause since the parties, being of equal bargaining power, were free to apportion the risks as they thought fit. The claimants, as owners of the premises, were in a better position to insure against the risk of fire.

POSITION OF THIRD PARTIES

As a result of the doctrine of privity (see Chapter 12), historically the courts have held a person who is not party to contract (a third party) is not protected by an exclusion clause in that contract, even if the clause purports to extend to him. Employees are regarded in this context as third parties; thus in *Cosgrove v Horsfall*, CA, 1945, a bus passenger was travelling under a free pass containing a clause that neither the bus authority nor its servants would be liable for injury. The passenger was injured as a result of the negligence of the bus driver. The driver was held liable in negligence as he was not a party to the contract containing the exclusion clause.

The decision was affirmed by the House of Lords in *Scruttons Ltd v Midland Silicones Ltd*, HL, 1962. Here a contract for the carriage of a drum of chemicals from the United States to England contained a clause limiting the liability of the carriers to $500. The drum was damaged through the negligence of a firm of stevedores whom the carriers had employed to unload the ship. It was held that the stevedores could not rely on the limitations clause contained in the contract between the carriers and the owners of the drum, to which they were not a party. The House also held that the stevedores could not rely on a similar limitation clause in the contract between the carriers and themselves, to which the owners were not a party.

The decision in Scruttons was avoided by the Privy Council in *New Zealand Shipping Co Ltd v A.M. Satterthwaite Co Ltd*, PC, 1975. Here it was held that the stevedore may take the benefit of the exclusion clause in a contract of carriage providing certain conditions are satisfied:

(1) the contract of carriage must make it clear that the stevedore is intended to be protected by the exclusion clause;

(2) the contract of carriage must make it clear that the carrier is contracting both on his own behalf and as agent for the stevedore;

(3) the stevedore must have authorised the carrier to contract in this way; and

(4) the stevedore must have provided consideration for the promise to exclude his liability.

In *Satterthwaite*, the consideration was held to consist in unloading the goods, which constituted the performance of an existing contractual duty owed to a third party, applying *Scotson v Pegg* (see Chapter 4). However, the somewhat elaborate device relied on in *Satterthwaite* may no longer be necessary now that the provisions of the Contracts (Rights of Third Parties) Act 1999 are in force (see Chapter 12). This permits the parties to contract on the basis that a third party may take the benefit of an exclusion clause.

LEGISLATION

The basic purpose of the Unfair Contract Terms Act, which was passed in 1977, is to restrict the extent to which liability in a contract can be excluded for breach of contract and negligence, largely by reference to the reasonableness requirement, but in some cases by a specific prohibition. Statutory control over unfair terms was extended by the Unfair Terms in Consumer Contracts Regulations 1999 which give effect to the EC Directive on Unfair Terms in Consumer Contracts (Directive 93/13).

The provisions of the Directive are to be contained in a separate piece of primary legislation—in Part 2 of the Consumer Rights Act 2014. The measures in the Unfair Contract Terms Act 1977 relating to consumer contracts will also be removed from the 1977 Act and be found in Part 1 of the Consumer Rights Act.

When the new Act has been brought into force, the 1977 Act will largely be concerned with business to business contracts.

The Unfair Contract Terms Act 1977

1. Scope

With the exception of implied terms in sale of goods and hire-purchase contracts (s.6), such terms in supply of goods and services contracts (s.7) and misrepresentation (s.8), the Act applies only to what is termed "business liability". This is defined by s.1(3) as liability arising from things done by a person in the course of a business or from the occupation of business premises.

There are certain types of contract to which the Act does not apply; these are listed in Sch.I and include contracts relating to the transfer of an interest in land and contracts of insurance.

2. Negligence

Liability for death or personal injury resulting from negligence cannot be excluded or restricted by any contract term or notice (s.2(1)). Any provision purporting to have this effect is, therefore, invalid. However, the exclusion or restriction of negligence liability for other loss or damage is permissible, but only in so far as the term or notice satisfies the requirement of reasonableness (s.2(2)). (As to "reasonableness", see below.)

3. Contractual liability

Where one party deals on the other party's written standard terms of business, then the other party cannot exclude or restrict his liability for breach of contract, except subject to the requirement of reasonableness (s.3(2)(a)). The reasonableness requirement is also extended to terms purporting to entitle the other party to render, (i) performance substantially different from that reasonably expected; or (ii) no performance at all (s.3(2)(b)).

In *Pegler v Wang*, 2000, the only clauses in the contract that were in standard form were the exclusion and limitation clauses themselves. The evidence showed that these clauses were, from the defendant's point of view, non-negotiable. The court held that the claimant had contracted on the defendant's "written standard terms of business" and therefore s.3 applied. It would seem, therefore, that it is not necessary for the contract as a whole to be in standard form, nor will it matter that one of the non-material clauses has been varied; *St Albans City and DC v International Computers Ltd*, CA, 1996; and *Watford Electronics Ltd v Sanderson CFL Ltd*, CA, 2001, at first instance, per Thornton J

As originally enacted, s.3 of the Unfair Contract Terms Act 1977 also applied where one party dealt "as consumer" but the Consumer Rights Act, when brought into force, will remove this provision from the Act of 1977 and it will fall under the consumer rights legislation.

4. Sale of goods and hire-purchase

In contracts for the sale of goods and hire-purchase, the implied terms as to title cannot be excluded or restricted by a contract term, whereas liability for breach of the implied terms as to correspondence with description or sample, fitness for purpose and merchantable quality can only be excluded or restricted in so far as the term satisfies the requirement of reasonableness (s.6). The provisions of s.6 are not confined to business liability but extend to liability arising under any contract of sale or hire-purchase

Under the 1977 Act as originally enacted, the implied terms relating to correspondence with description or sample, fitness for purpose and satis-factory quality could not be excluded as against a person dealing as con-sumer. The Consumer Rights Act, when brought into force, will transfer this provision to the consumer rights legislation.

It seems that in order to exclude or restrict liability (in business to business transactions) for breach of implied conditions such as those in s.14 of the Sale of Goods Act 1979, some express reference to "conditions" may be advisable; *Bominflot mbH & Co v Petroplus Marketing AG*, CA, 2010.

There are similar provisions relating to implied terms in contracts for the supply of goods and services in s.7. The implied terms as to title cannot be excluded in a contract for work and materials, whereas in contracts of hire they can be excluded, but only insofar as the clause satisfies the requirement of reasonableness.

5. Reasonableness

LEGISLATION HIGHLIGHTER

The Unfair Contract Terms Act 1977 s.11(1) provides that where a term must satisfy the requirement of reasonableness, the test is that the term shall have been a fair and reasonable one to be included having regard to the circumstances which were, or ought reasonably to have been, known to, or in the contemplation of, the parties when the contract was made.

Where the reasonableness requirement must be met in the case of a limitation clause, the court's attention is drawn to, (i) the resources available to meet the liability; and (ii) the extent to which insurance cover was open to the party purporting to limit liability (s.11(4)).

No further guidance is provided by the Act except that, in relation to clauses excluding liability for breach of the implied terms in sale of goods, etc. contracts (those governed by ss.6–7) certain guidelines are laid down in Sch.2. It is clear that these guidelines will be looked at in other types of contract and therefore their importance cannot be underestimated. The guidelines are, so far as appear to the court to be relevant, as follows:

(a) the strength of the bargaining positions of the parties relative to each other, taking into account the availability of another source of supply;

(b) whether the customer received an inducement to agree to the term, e.g. where goods are offered more cheaply with an exclusion clause but more expensively without; *R.W. Green Ltd v Cade Bros Farms*, 1978;

(c) whether the customer ought to have known the existence and extent of the term. This would appear to refer to knowledge and awareness of the clause via trade custom and previous dealings;

(d) where the term excludes or restricts any relevant liability if some condition is not complied with, whether it was reasonable at the time of the contract to expect that compliance with that condition would be practicable. In *Green v Cade*, seed potatoes were delivered on terms that any notice of rejection or complaint must be made within three days of delivery. The clause was held unreasonable in relation to a defect not discoverable on inspection at the time of delivery;

(e) whether the goods were manufactured, processed or adapted to the special order of the customer.

Further judicial guidance as to reasonableness has been provided by *George Mitchell (Chesterhall) Ltd v Finney Lock Seeds Ltd*, HL, 1983, which was decided under the similar provisions of s.55 of the Sale of Goods Act 1979. Lord Bridge, in referring to the trial judge's decision as to whether a clause is reasonable, said:

> "There will sometimes be room for legitimate difference of judicial opinion ... the appellate court should treat the original decision with the utmost respect and refrain from interference with it unless satisfied that it proceeded on some erroneous principle or was plainly and obviously wrong."

In this case, the defendants supplied the claimant farmers with cabbage seed for £201. The contract contained a clause that if the seeds were defective, liability would be limited to the replacement of the seed or refunding the price. The crop failed owing to the seeds being unsatisfactory and the claimants suffered loss amounting to £61,000. The House of Lords upheld the unanimous decision of the Court of Appeal that it would not be fair and reasonable to allow reliance on the clause.

KEY CASE

SMITH V ERIC S BUSH, HL, 1989

It was held that a disclaimer of liability used by surveyors in relation to building society valuations was unreasonable. Lord Griffiths said that there were four questions which should always be considered in deciding on the issue of reasonableness:

(1) Were the parties of equal bargaining power?
(2) In the case of advice, would it have been reasonably practical to obtain the advice from an alternative source taking into account considerations of cost and time?
(3) How difficult is the task being undertaken for which liability is being excluded?
(4) What are the practical consequences of the decision on unreasonableness?

Comment

With regard to question (3) above, it seems that the more difficult or dangerous the task, the more reasonable it may be to exclude or limit liability. Question (4) involves consideration of the sums of money potentially at stake and the ability of the parties to bear the loss involved. In this respect, the availability and cost of insurance is a relevant factor when deciding which party should be required to bear the risk of loss.

An illustration of the stance of the courts to exclusion clauses in commercial contracts is to be found in *Watford Electronics Ltd v Sanderson CFL Ltd*, CA, 2001. Here clauses of exclusion and limitation in a computer software and hardware contract were upheld by the Court of Appeal as reasonable, reversing the decision of the trial judge. The court stressed that the contract had been negotiated between experienced businessmen of equal bargaining power and skill. Unless satisfied that one party had effectively taken unfair advantage of the other, or that a term was so unreasonable as plainly not to have been understood or considered, the court should not interfere (per Chadwick LJ).

Gibson LJ adopted the dictum of Forbes J in *Salvage Association v CAP Financial Services*, 1995, where he said:

> "Generally speaking, where a party well able to look after itself enters into a commercial contract and, with full knowledge of all relevant circumstances, willingly accepts the terms of the contract which provides for apportionment of the financial risks of that transaction, I think it is very likely that those terms will be held to be fair and reasonable."

This approach was applied by the Court of Appeal in *Regus (UK) Ltd v Epcot Solutions Ltd*, CA, 2008. Such sentiments appear to cast the Act of 1977 (as originally enacted) as an essentially a consumer protection measure since the scope for clauses in commercial contracts negotiated on equal terms to be struck down would appear to be extremely limited.

Unfair Terms in Consumer Contracts

The EC Directive on Unfair Terms in Consumer Contracts (Directive 93/13) was originally transposed into domestic legislation by the Unfair Terms in Consumer Contracts Regulations 1994. These regulations were replaced by the 1999 regulations which came into force on October 1, 1999. But these regulations are to be revoked when the Consumer Rights Act is fully brought into force. The provisions of the Directive will be implemented by Part 2 of the Act.

1 Introduction

Before considering the provisions of Part 2, it should first be noted that, under the Act, traders in "consumer contracts" will not be able exclude or restrict the consumer's statutory rights, such as liability for breach of terms corresponding to the implied terms in sale of goods contracts relating to title, description, fitness for purpose, satisfactory quality and sales by sample. Any term in a consumer contract purporting to exclude or restrict such liability will

Figure 13: The Operation of the Unfair Contract Terms Act 1977 as Originally Enacted

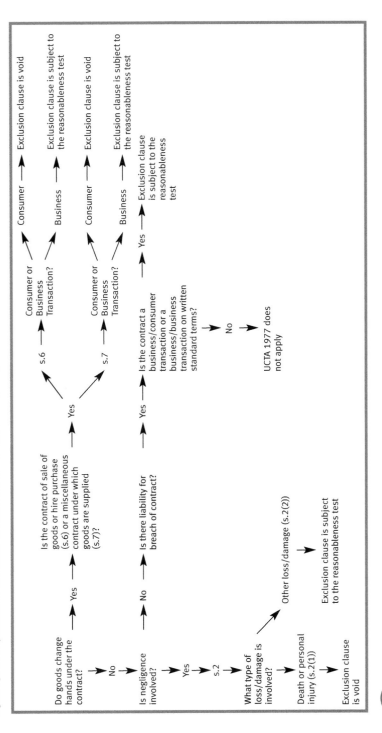

Figure 14: The Operation of the Unfair Contract Terms Act 1977 after Amendment by the Reform under the Consumer Rights Legislation

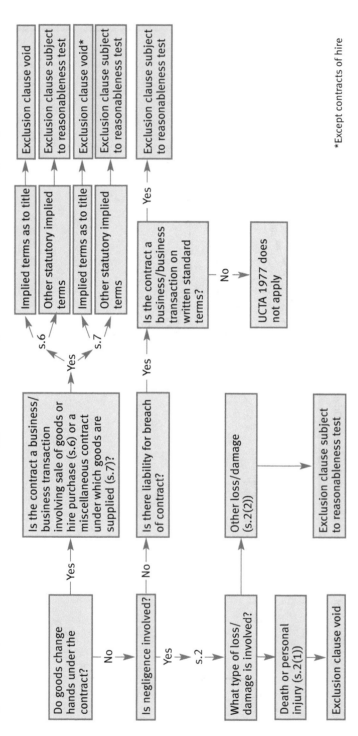

*Except contracts of hire

be void, as will be terms making it more difficult and onerous for consumers to exercise their rights; or placing them at a disadvantage after doing so. With specified exceptions, a trader in a consumer contract or consumer notice, will not be able to exclude or restrict liability for death or personal injury resulting from negligence. Such terms are void.

2 Scope
Part 2 of the Act applies to unfair terms in certain contracts concluded between a trader and a consumer—"consumer contracts" (see Chapter 6). It also applies to non-contractual consumer notices. The burden of proving that an individual is not a consumer falls on the trader. The provisions do not apply to contracts of employment.

3 Effect
An unfair term will not binding on the consumer. Whether a term is unfair must be decided by reference to the nature of the subject-matter, all the circumstances existing when the term was agreed, and all of the other terms of the contract. When a term in a consumer contract is not binding as a result of the application of the fairness assessment, the contract will continue, so far as practicable, to have effect in every other respect.

4 The assessment of fairness
A trader must ensure that a written term of a consumer contract or consumer notice will be transparent. If a term is ambiguous, the meaning most favourable to the consumer is to prevail.

> **LEGISLATION HIGHLIGHTER**
>
> A term or notice will be "unfair" if, contrary to the requirement of good faith, it causes a significant imbalance in the parties' rights and obligations to the detriment of the consumer.

To assist in assessing fairness, Schedule 2, Part 1 of the Act contains *an indicative and non-exhaustive* list of terms which may be regarded as unfair (the "Grey List").
   The examples in the list include the following:
   (1) a term having the object or effect of making an agreement binding on the consumer in a case where the provision of services by the trader is subject to a condition whose realization depends on the trader's will alone
   (2) a term having the object or effect of requiring a consumer who fails to fulfil his obligations under the contract to pay a disproportionately high sum in compensation

(3) a term having the object or effect of irrevocably binding the consumer to terms which the consumer has had no real opportunity of becoming acquainted before the conclusion of the contract

(4) a term having the object or effect of enabling the trader to alter unilaterally without a valid reason any characteristics of the goods, digital content or services to be provided

5 Exemption from the test of fairness

A term in a consumer contract may not be assessed for fairness to the extent that (a) it specifies the main subject-matter of the contract, or (b) the assessment is of the appropriateness of the price payable under the contract by comparison with the goods, digital content or services supplied under it.

A term will only be exempt from the assessment of fairness if it is transparent and prominent. The exemption does not apply to terms listed in Part 1 of Schedule 2 (see above).

6 Enforcement

Under the Act, the Competition and Markets Authority ("CMA", replacing the Office of Fair Trading) and other specified regulators may investigate and seek injunctions to prevent the use of terms which are unfair, non-transparent or void under the above-discussed provisions. In addition the new CMA may collate and publicize information about actions taken against unfair terms. If appropriate, the CMA may also provide guidance.

An action commenced by the Director General for Fair Trading under the unfair terms legislation came before the House of Lords in the following case.

KEY CASE

DIRECTOR GENERAL OF FAIR TRADING V FIRST NATIONAL BANK, HL, 2001
The case concerned a term in the bank's standard form loan agreement. The term provided that, where the borrower was in default and the bank had obtained a court judgment for the amount due, interest at the contract rate continued to be payable until the judgment was discharged, despite the fact that all the instalments due under the judgment had been paid. The Director General sought an injunction to restrain the use of the standard term on the ground that it was unfair; this application was successful in the Court of Appeal. The Bank appealed.

Held: The clause was not unfair as it did not cause a significant imbalance in the parties' rights and obligations to the detriment of the consumer in a manner contrary to the requirement of good faith.

Comment

Despite the unpleasant shock that the term might give to consumers, it was considered legitimate, because without it, the Bank would be unable to charge interest but would not have recovered all of its money until the entire balance on the borrower's account had been repaid.

REVISION CHECKLIST

You should now know and understand:

- [ ] **the rules of incorporation;**
- [ ] **the rules of construction;**
- [ ] **the application of the Unfair Contract Terms Act 1977.**

QUESTION AND ANSWER

THE QUESTION

Harriet is a partner in an accountancy firm and she regularly travels by train to visit clients in connection with auditing their accounts. On one such occasion, she took her suitcase to be deposited at the left luggage office of the North Midland Rail Company.

Harriet was handed a small slip of paper which she was told by the attendant was to enable her to reclaim her suitcase. Harriet put the slip of paper in her handbag without glancing at it. On the paper appeared the following words: "The liability of the company for loss of or damage to goods deposited is limited to £50 or the value of the said goods, whichever the lower."

These words also appeared on a notice above the left luggage office counter. Harriet's suitcase contained a laptop computer worth £500. When she returned to collect the suitcase the attendant informed her that it was missing and could not be found.

Advise Harriet.

LIVERPOOL JOHN MOORES UNIVERSITY
LEARNING SERVICES

General guidance

Exclusion clauses is a multi-layered topic that contains long-established common law principles and more recent statutory regulation. You can expect a problem question to require a consideration of both elements.

In terms of approach it is advisable to apply the common law rules first. You will need to analyse the facts and consider whether the particular clause has been incorporated into the contract. Remember here that a clause may be incorporated by signature, by notice or by previous dealings. With regard to the latter, the facts may say no more than the claimant "has had dealings in the past" with the party purporting to rely on the clause (see, for example the wording of the question above).

You must then consider the construction of the clause. Remember here that the cases are of limited value as precedents and, since the passing of the Unfair Contract Terms Act 1977, the courts no longer need to resort to "strained" construction to restrict the operation of exclusion clauses. This means that there is currently a much less strict approach to construction and many of the older cases should be viewed with caution on this issue. It is also the case that limitation clauses are construed much less stringently than exclusion clauses. In *Ailsa Craig Fishing Co Ltd v Malvern Fishing Co Ltd*, HL, 1983, Lord Fraser confirmed that there was no reason why "limitation clauses should be judged by the specially exacting standards which are applied to exclusion ... clauses".

Turning to the Unfair Contract Terms Act 1977, it is important to identify the correct operative section, i.e. s.2 (negligence); s.3 (breach of contract); s.6 (implied terms in sale of goods, etc contracts); or s.7 (implied terms in other contracts under which goods pass). In this context a useful initial question is to ask: do goods change hands under the contract? In those cases where the clause has to satisfy the requirement of reasonableness in s.11, it will be appropriate to apply the guidelines in Sch.2 of the Act.

In the case of unfair terms in consumer contracts, the provisions of Part 2 of the Consumer Rights Act (when brought into force) will apply rather than those of the Unfair Contract Terms Act.

Model answer

If Harriet is to recover full compensation from the rail company, it has to be shown that the limitation clause cannot be relied on by the company. The courts have developed a number of weapons to use against clauses excluding or restricting liability, and in addition the Unfair Contract Terms Act 1977 may require the clause to satisfy the requirement of reasonableness.

The first question that must be asked here is whether the limitation clause is incorporated into the contract. The courts require such a clause to be contained in a contractual document, i.e. a document which the reasonable person would expect to contain contractual terms; *Chapelton v Barry UDC*, CA, 1940. On the facts given, it may be doubted whether one would expect to find contractual terms on the slip of paper handed to Harriet.

A further requirement is that reasonable and sufficient notice of the clause must be given before or at the time of the contract; *Olley v Marlborough Court*, CA, 1949. It may be that the notice situated over the counter, if sufficiently prominent, will serve this purpose. Further, even if there has been insufficient notice on this occasion, Harriet might be bound by a regular and consistent course of previous dealings; *Spurling v Bradshaw*, CA, 1956. It is stated that she "regularly travels by train". If she has travelled with this company and deposited luggage on a significant number of occasions in the past she may be bound by the clause.

Even if the clause is incorporated under the above rules, the court will apply certain rules of construction to see whether the clause clearly and unambiguously covers the breach which has taken place. Under the contra proferentem rule, the clause will be construed as narrowly as possible against the party who has inserted it and purports to rely on it. In particular, very clear words are required to exclude or restrict liability for negligence. Here, there is no express reference to negligence and in such a case the court may ask whether there is any other head of liability the words could cover; *White v John Warwick Co Ltd*, CA, 1953. In that case, general words of exclusion were held not to apply to negligence since the defendants were also under strict liability for breach of contract. However, in *Alderslade v Hendon Laundry Ltd*, CA, 1945, handkerchiefs were sent for laundering under a limitation clause referring merely to loss or damage.

The clause was held to apply since if it did not apply to negligence it would lack subject-matter since there was no other head of liability to which it could possibly refer. In that case, the safekeeping of the goods was an ancillary obligation under the contract, whereas in the present case it is the very purpose of the contract itself. Since it is not clear how the suitcase has been lost (e.g. negligence or deliberate misdelivery), the court may conclude the clause to be insufficiently clear to limit liability for the loss of the suitcase. Support for this view is to be found in *Woolmer v Delmer Price Ltd*, 1955, although that case involved a total exclusion clause rather than a limitation clause. Finally, on the issue of construction, it is clear that the courts now view limitation clauses less strictly than exclusion clauses and the House of Lords has held that the rules of construction should not be applied to limitation clauses with the same rigour as exclusion clauses; *Ailsa Craig Fishing Co v Malvern Fishing Co*, HL, 1983.

The contract is subject to the Unfair Contract Terms Act 1977 and as such the clause must satisfy the requirement of reasonableness in s.11 of the Act, as applied by s.2(2). The test is that the term shall have been a fair and reasonable one to be included, having regard to all the circumstances known or contemplated or which ought reasonably to have been known or contemplated by the parties when the contract was made. In the case of limitation clauses, the court must look at the resources which could be expected to be available to meet the liability and the extent to which insurance cover was open (s.11(4)).

In addition, certain guidelines are laid down by Sch.2 to the Act that may well be referred to, although strictly they are intended for sale of goods and hire-purchase contracts. Thus it may be relevant to ask whether the parties are of equal bargaining power (probably not); whether the railway company was a monopoly supplier; and whether Harriet should have known of the existence and extent of the term through previous dealings. It is possible to argue that the clause in this case is reasonable as the company has no means of knowing what valuables may be inside suitcases deposited with them. In the circumstances, it might not be reasonable for the risk of insurance to lie with the railway company. Indeed, it may be impossible for them to obtain cover at a reasonable cost. Harriet would therefore be best advised to attempt to avoid the clause through the tests of incorporation and construction.

As Harriet appears not to be a consumer in relation to this contract, the provisions of the consumer rights legislation will not apply. In entering the contract, she is acting for purposes wholly within her business or profession; thus it is not therefore a "consumer contract".

Misrepresentation

INTRODUCTION

We are concerned in this chapter with the circumstances in which a contract may be avoided on the grounds of an actionable misrepresentation. This involves an examination of:

1   The meaning of "actionable misrepresentation"
2   The types of misrepresentation: fraudulent, negligent and wholly innocent
3   The remedy of rescission for misrepresentation
4   The remedy of damages for misrepresentation
5   The exclusion of liability for misrepresentation

A statement made during negotiations may, as we have seen, become incorporated into the contract as a term. Alternatively, the statement may form the basis of a collateral contract or it may be a mere representation (see Chapter 6).

If the statement is a contractual term or a collateral contract the remedy for non-compliance is an action for breach of contract. If a mere representation proves false, the remedy will, in most cases, lie in an action for rescission and/or damages for misrepresentation, the subject-matter of this chapter.

An actionable representation renders the contract voidable, i.e. valid until avoided. The definition of actionable misrepresentation, the types of misrepresentation and the remedies available will be considered in this chapter.

ACTIONABLE MISREPRESENTATION

CHECKPOINT

An "actionable misrepresentation" may be defined as *a false statement of fact* made by one party to the other, which, whilst not being a term of the contract, *induces* the other party to enter the contract. The two elements in italics in the preceding sentence will be considered below.

False Statement of Fact

It seems that a statement will be "false" if not "substantially" correct; *Avon Insurance Ltd v Swire Fraser Ltd*, 2000.

An actionable misrepresentation is a false statement of some specific existing fact or past event and as a result the following are excluded, i.e. do not amount to misrepresentation if false.

1. Statements of future conduct or intention.

A false statement by a person as to what they will do in the future is not misrepresentation; for example, the company prospectus that falsely states that over the next four years, the company will invest a billion pounds. If, however, the statement of intention is a wilful lie, then it may amount to a misrepresentation of fact, as illustrated by the following case.

KEY CASE

EDGINGTON V FITZMAURICE, CA, 1885

Company directors raised money from the public by stating that the money would be used to expand the business. In fact, their real intention was to use the money to pay off the company's existing debt.

Held: The statement was a (fraudulent) misrepresentation of fact. The directors had misrepresented their state of mind—they had lied about their intentions.

Comment

In this case, Bowen LJ famously said: "[T]he state of a man's mind is as much a fact as the state of his digestion." He added that, although it is difficult to prove what the state of a person's mind is, if it can be ascertained, it is as much of a fact as anything else.

2. Statements of belief or opinion.

A false statement of opinion is not a misrepresentation of fact. In *Bisset v Wilkinson*, PC, 1927, the owner of a farm, which had never before been used as a sheep farm, stated to a prospective purchaser that he believed it would support 2,000 sheep. This was held to be a statement of opinion, not fact.

As with statements of intention (above), if the opinion is not honestly held, there may be a misrepresentation of fact; *Edgington v Fitzmaurice*. Further, if the maker of the statement possesses special knowledge or skill in relation to the subject-matter or is in a stronger position to know the truth, then a statement expressed as an opinion may be held to be an implied misrepresentation of fact; *Smith v Land and House Property Corp*, CA, 1884. "Mere puff" (see Chapter 3) cannot amount to misrepresentation.

3. Statements of law.

The traditional rule was that a false statement as to what the law is could not be an actionable misrepresentation. The difficulty of distinguishing between a statement of law and a statement of fact is illustrated by *Solle v Butcher*, CA, 1950, where a statement that a flat was "new" and therefore not subject to the Rent Restriction Acts, was held to be a statement of fact.

It would seem that now, however, a misrepresentation of law can constitute actionable misrepresentation; *Pankhania v London Borough of Hackney*, 2002. In so deciding, the High Court was following the ruling of the House of Lords in *Kleinwort Benson Ltd v Lincoln City Council*, HL, 1999 that money paid under a mistake of law could be recovered.

4. Silence or non-disclosure.

The general rule is that to remain silent does not amount to misrepresentation. An example of the rule is *Hands v Simpson Fawcett*, 1928. In this case it was held that a commercial traveller who failed to disclose at a job interview that he had had serious motoring convictions made no misrepresentation. He was under no duty, in the circumstances, to disclose them. The rule is a general one and the court is free to conclude that a duty of disclosure arises in particular circumstances; *Sybron Corporation v Rockhem Ltd*, CA, 1983.

The rule is subject to the following established exceptions:

(a) Where the statement is a half-truth. A statement that does not present the whole truth may be regarded as a misrepresentation; thus if A, whilst giving credit reference concerning B, states that B is honest and trustworthy but does not disclose that B has been bankrupt, A may be regarded as making a misrepresentation; *Tapp v Lee*, 1803.

(b) Where a statement was true when made but, due to a change of circumstances, has become false by the time it is acted upon. In *With v O'Flanagan*, CA, 1936, the vendor of a medical practice truthfully stated to a prospective purchaser that it was worth £2,000 per annum. The vendor then fell ill, so that, by the time the contract was signed four months later, the receipts had fallen to almost nothing. It was held that the failure of the vendor to disclose this state of affairs to the purchaser amounted to a misrepresentation.

(c) Contracts uberrimae fidei, i.e. of the utmost good faith. In this class of contracts, there is a duty to disclose all the material facts as one party is in a strong position to know the truth.

The leading example is contracts of insurance, where there is a duty on the insured to disclose every circumstance which would influence the judgment of the prudent insurer in fixing the premium or deciding whether they will take the risk. Such contracts are voidable.

(d) Parties in a fiduciary relationship. Where such a relationship exists between the parties to a contract, a duty of disclosure will arise, e.g. principal and agent; solicitor and client; partner and partner; doctor and patient.

It is possible to have a misrepresentation purely by conduct. In *Spice Girls v Aprilia World Service BV*, CA, 2002, the defendants agreed to sponsor a Spice Girls tour. The group had appeared in promotional material before the contract was concluded when they knew that one of their number, Geri Halliwell, was about to leave the group. It was held that there had been misrepresentation by conduct.

The Meaning of Inducement

To amount to a misrepresentation, the false statement must induce the contract. To operate as an inducement, the statement must fulfil the following requirements:

1. The statement must be addressed to the party misled.
In *Peek v Gurney*, HL, 1873, the appellant purchased shares on the faith of a misrepresentation which in fact was intended to mislead a different class of purchaser from that to which the appellant belonged. The House of Lords held that the appellant's action for misrepresentation must fail.

However, if it can be shown that the maker of the statement knew that the statement would be passed on to the claimant, then the maker of the statement will be liable in misrepresentation; *Pilmore v Hood*, 1838. This principle was applied by the Court of Appeal in *Clef Acquitaine SARL v Laporte Materials (Barrow) Ltd*, CA, 2000.

The fact that a representation can be of a continuing nature and remain in force until the relevant contract is concluded was confirmed in *Cramaso LLP v Ogilvie-Grant, Earl of Stansfield*, SC, 2014. This will depend on the representor's conduct demonstrating—expressly or impliedly—that the representation was intended to continue in force and be actionable even though the original representee turns out not to be an ultimate party to the contract.

2. The statement must be the actual inducement.
The requirement of materiality is not objective; i.e. whether the misrepresentation would have influenced a reasonable person is of evidentiary value but it is not the determining factor; *Museprime Properties Ltd v Adhill Properties*, 1990. However, if the claimant relies on his or her own judgment or investigations, there will be no liability on the part of the misrepresentor. In *Attwood v Small*, HL, 1838, purchasers of a mine were told exaggerated

statements as to its earning capacity by the vendors. The purchasers had these statements checked by their own expert agents, who (in error) reported them as correct. It was held that the claimants had been induced to enter the contract by their agents' report and not by the vendors.

If the claimant has a misrepresentation made to him or her and then is offered the means of discovering the truth, but does not take the offer up, the misrepresentation may still be considered as an inducement.

KEY CASE

REDGRAVE V HURD, CA, 1881

The claimant, vendor of a law practice, stated to the defendant purchaser that the income was £300 per annum, and the claimant showed papers to the defendant was which purported to prove this. The defendant did not read them. The defendant agreed a sale but found that the practice was worthless; the claimant then sought to enforce the sale.

Held: The claimant could not do so, as there had been an actionable misrepresentation. It was immaterial that the misrepresentee had the means of discovering the truth and might with reasonable diligence have discovered it.

Comment

This case involved an action for rescission brought at a time when damages could not be awarded for non-fraudulent misrepresentation. Now that damages are available for negligent misrepresentation, it is possible that damages may be reduced on the basis of the misrepresentee's contributory negligence in not examining relevant documents (but that should not, per se, prevent rescission); *Gran Gelato Ltd v Richcliff (Group) Ltd*, 1992.

Further, if the claimant is unaware of the misrepresentation at the time of entering the contract, there can be no liability (*Horsfall v Thomas*, 1862), and likewise, though he was aware of it, it is proved that it cannot possibly have affected his judgment; *Smith v Chadwick*, HL, 1884.

To be actionable, the misrepresentation does not have to be the sole factor inducing the claimant to enter the contract; *Edgington v Fitzmaurice*, CA, 1885.

TYPES OF MISREPRESENTATION

In the modern law, misrepresentation is classed as fraudulent, negligent or wholly innocent. These are considered below.

Fraudulent Misrepresentation

"Fraudulent" in this sense was defined by Lord Herschell in *Derry v Peek*, HL, 1889 as a false statement that is "made (i) knowingly, or (ii) without belief in its truth, or (iii) recklessly, careless as to whether it be true or false". The essence of fraud is absence of honest belief; in *Derry v Peek*, a share prospectus falsely stated that the company had the right to use mechanical power to draw trams, without explaining that governmental consent was required for this. In fact, the directors honestly believed that obtaining consent was a pure formality, although it was ultimately refused. The House of Lords held that there had been no fraudulent misrepresentation.

Negligent Misrepresentation

Negligent misrepresentation consists of two types:

1. Negligent misstatement at common law.
Until 1963, damages could only be claimed for misrepresentation where it was fraudulent. All non-fraudulent misrepresentations were classed as "innocent" and damages were not available for such innocent misrepresentations. In 1963, the House of Lords stated, obiter, in *Hedley Byrne Co Ltd v Heller Partners Ltd*, HL, 1964, that in certain circumstances damages may be recoverable in tort for negligent misstatement causing financial loss. The liability depends on a duty of care arising from a "special relationship" between the parties. It is now clear that a party can claim damages under the principle in *Hedley Byrne* where a negligent misstatement has induced him or her to enter a contract; *Esso Petroleum Co Ltd v Mardon*, CA, 1976. Broadly speaking, the special relationship will only arise where the maker of the statement possesses knowledge or skill relevant to the subject-matter of the contract and can reasonably foresee that the other party will rely on the statement.

2. Negligent misrepresentation under the Misrepresentation Act 1967.

Section 2(1) of the Misrepresentation Act 1967 introduced, for the first time, a statutory claim for damages for non-fraudulent misrepresentation. Section 2(1) provides that where a person has entered a contract after a misrepresentation has been made to them by another party thereto, and, as a result thereof, they have suffered loss, then, if the person making the misrepresentation would be liable to damages in respect thereof had the misrepresentation been made fraudulently, that person shall be so liable notwithstanding that the misrepresentation was not made fraudulently, unless they prove that they had reasonable ground to believe and did believe, up to the time the contract was made, that the facts represented were true. It should be noted that the sub-section assumes all non-fraudulent statements to be negligent and puts the burden on the maker of the statement to disprove negligence.

Wholly Innocent Misrepresentation

We have seen that, before 1963, the word "innocent" was used to describe all misrepresentations that were not fraudulent. In the light of *Hedley Byrne* and s.2(1) of the Act of 1967, the word innocent may now be used to refer to a statement made by a person who has reasonable grounds for believing in its truth. To avoid confusion, "wholly innocent" is a better description.

REMEDIES FOR MISREPRESENTATION

Once an actionable misrepresentation is established, it becomes necessary to consider the remedies available to the misrepresentee. The remedies are as follows.

Rescission

Rescission, i.e. setting aside the contract, is possible whether the misrepresentation is fraudulent, negligent or wholly innocent.

Where a contract is rescinded it is terminated ab initio; the object is to put the parties back in the position they would have been in had the contract never been made. The injured party may elect to rescind the contract. This can be done by notifying the other party or by any other act indicating repudiation of liability, e.g. notifying the authorities; *Car and Universal Finance Co Ltd v Caldwell*, CA, 1964. The injured party may also apply to the court for an order of rescission.

An order of rescission may be accompanied by the court ordering an indemnity. This is a money payment by the misrepresentor to restore the parties to their position as if the contract had never been made. An indemnity is payable in respect of obligations necessarily created by the contract and it should be distinguished from damages. The distinction is illustrated by *Whittington v Seale-Hayne*, 1900. The claimants bred poultry and took a lease of the defendant's premises, as a result of a wholly innocent mis-representation that the premises were sanitary. In fact, the water supply was poisoned and the defendants submitted to rescission. The claimants requested an indemnity to cover:

(i)   loss of profits;
(ii) value of stock lost;
(iii) removal costs;
(iv) medical expenses;
(v)   rent and rates; and
(vi) the cost of repairs ordered by the local council.

It was held that an indemnity would be awarded in respect of items (v) and (vi) only, as these were obligations necessarily created by the contract. As the claimants were not obliged to carry on a business, items (i)–(iv), had they been awarded, would have amounted to an award of damages.

The power to award an indemnity is not affected by the Mis-representation Act 1967, although it will not be applicable where damages are in fact awarded. Thus, the remedy remains particularly significant where the contract is rescinded for a wholly innocent misrepresentation.

Bars to Rescission
The injured party may lose the right to rescind in the following circumstances ("bars to rescission").

1. Affirmation
The injured party will affirm the contract if, with full knowledge of the mis-representation and of his right to rescind, they expressly state that they intend to continue with it, or if they perform an act from which the intention may be implied; *Long v Lloyd*, CA, 1958; *Peyman v Lanjani*, CA, 1985.

Lapse of time may be evidence of affirmation, although where the misrepresentation is fraudulent, the time which is evidence of affirmation runs from the time when the fraud was, or with reasonable diligence could have been discovered. There is authority that in the case of non-fraudulent misrepresentation, time runs from the date of the contract, not the date of discovery of the misrepresentation; *Leaf v International Galleries*, CA, 1950.

2. Impossibility of restitution

The injured party will lose the right to rescind if the parties cannot be restored to their original position. In *Vigers v Pike*, 1842, a lease of a mine which had been entered into as a result of a misrepresentation could not be rescinded as there had been considerable extraction of minerals since the date of the contract.

It should be noted that precise restoration is not required and the remedy is still available if substantial restoration is possible; *Erlanger v New Sombrero Phosphate Co*, HL, 1873; and *Halpern v Halpern*, CA, 2007. Deterioration in the value or condition of property is not a bar to rescission; *Armstrong v Jackson*, 1917.

3. Third party rights

Rescission cannot be ordered where third party rights have accrued, bona fide and for value. Thus, if A obtains goods from B by misrepresentation and sells them to C, who takes in good faith, B cannot later rescind on learning of the misrepresentation in order to recover the goods from C; *White v Garden*, 1851.

Two further bars to rescission were abolished by s.1 of the Misrepresentation Act 1967, namely where the misrepresentation had become incorporated as a contractual term and where, after a non-fraudulent misrepresentation, the contract had been executed.

Damages for Misrepresentation

Damages for misrepresentation may be claimed or awarded under the following heads.

1. Damages for fraudulent misrepresentation

The claim for such damages is a claim in the tort of deceit. The object is to restore the claimant to the position they would have been in had the representation not been made, i.e. the amount by which the claimant is out of pocket by entering the contract; *McConnel v Wright*, CA, 1903. The "out of pocket" rule does not necessarily preclude a claim for loss of profits as illustrated by the following case.

KEY CASE

EAST V MAURER, CA, 1991
The claimants purchased a hairdressing salon business from the defendant as a result of a fraudulent representation by the defendant that he would not normally be working at his other salon nearby. He continued to work there and consequently the claimants' salon was never profitable. They sued for loss of profits.

Held: Damages would be awarded for the profit the claimant might have made had he bought a different salon in the same area, i.e. he could recover for the "opportunity cost" of relying on the misrepresentation

Comment
The damages in this case were awarded on the tortious basis, i.e. putting the parties back in the position they would have been in had the representation not been made. Such damages will be more modest than if damages were awarded on the contractual "loss of bargain" basis (see Chapter 14).

It seems that the test of remoteness in deceit is that the claimant may recover for all the direct loss incurred as a result of the fraudulent inducement, regardless of foreseeability; *Doyle v Olby (Ironmongers) Ltd*, CA, 1969, affirmed by the House of Lords in *Smith New Court Securities Ltd v Scrimgeour Vickers (Asset Management) Ltd*, HL, 1996.

2. Damages for negligent misrepresentation
The claimant may elect to claim damages under the principle in *Hedley Byrne v Heller*, HL, 1963 providing the ingredients of the tort are established. The award of damages under *Hedley Byrne* differs from damages in deceit only in that, under *Hedley Byrne*, the remoteness test is that of reasonable foreseeability.

Alternatively the claimant may claim damages for negligent misrepresentation under s.2(1) of the Act of 1967 and where the claimant has entered a contract as a result of the misrepresentation this will be the normal course to pursue, as opposed to an action in tort. Under s.2(1), the maker of the statement is assumed to have no reasonable grounds for believing in the truth of the statement and bears the burden of disproving this. This is the most significant advantage of a claim under s.2(1) over *Hedley Byrne*.

The fact that the maker of the statement bears a heavy burden of proof under s.2(1) is illustrated by *Howard Marine and Dredging Co Ltd v A. Ogden and Sons (Excavations) Ltd*, CA, 1978. Here, in negotiations to hire out two sea-going barges, the owners' representative misrepresented the carrying capacity of the barges. He relied on Lloyds Register which was in fact incorrect; the correct information was on file at the owners' head office. The Court of Appeal held that there was liability under s.2(1); the assumption contained in s.2(1) had not been disproved.

Royscot Trust Ltd v Rogerson, CA, 1991 established that damages under s.2(1) are to be assessed on the same basis as fraudulent misrepresentation, although doubts were expressed as to this in the *Smith New Court Securities* case (above). Indeed, this so-called "fiction of fraud" under s.2(1) has caused some controversy, since the remoteness rule for fraud (discussed above), can produce a very high level of damages for what is essentially negligence, not fraud. This was acknowledged by Rix J in *Avon Insurance Ltd v Swire Fraser Ltd*, 2000, where he said the courts should not be too willing to find a negligent misrepresentation where there was room for the exercise of judgment. In *Gran Gelato v Richcliff (Group) Ltd*, 1992 it was held that where there were concurrent claims against a party under s.2(1) and *Hedley Byrne*, damages awarded for both could be reduced by reason of the contributory negligience of the claimant—however this has no application to actions in fraud; *Alliance and Leicester Building Society v Edgestop Ltd*, 1994.

3. Damages in lieu of rescission
It is clear that damages may not be claimed for a wholly innocent misrepresentation, i.e. one that is neither fraudulent or negligent. The only remedy for wholly innocent misrepresentation is rescission, which may be accompanied by an indemnity.

The previous paragraph is subject to the following. Section 2(2) of the Misrepresentation Act 1967 gives the court a discretion, where the injured party would be entitled to rescind, to award damages in lieu of rescission. Damages under s.2(2) cannot be claimed as such; they can only be awarded by the court. The power of the court under the sub-section can only be used in the case of non-fraudulent (i.e. negligent and wholly innocent) misrepresentation. It had always been assumed that the loss of the right to rescind (e.g. by affirmation) would remove this power to award damages, however this was not accepted in *Thomas Witter Ltd v TBP Industries*, 1996. Later cases have come to the opposite conclusion; *Government of Zanzibar v British Aerospace Ltd*, 2000. Further, the measure of damages under s.2(2) was considered in *William Sindall Plc v Cambridgeshire CC*, CA, 1994, where Evans LJ suggested that it should be "the difference in value between what the [claimant] was misled into believing he was acquiring, and the value of what he in fact received".

Where damages are awarded under s.2(1), the court must (by virtue of s.2(3)) take into account any damages awarded in lieu of rescission under s.2(2).

EXCLUSION OF LIABILITY FOR MISREPRESENTATION

Section 3 of the Misrepresentation Act 1967, as amended by s.8 of the Unfair Contract Terms Act 1977, provides that if a contract contains a term which would exclude or restrict:

(1) any liability to which a party to a contract may be subject by reason of any misrepresentation made by him or her before the contract was made; or

(2) any remedy available to another party to the contract by reason of such a misrepresentation, that term shall be of no effect except in so far as it satisfies the requirement of reasonableness as stated in s.11(1) of the Unfair Contract Terms Act 1977 (see Chapter 6); and it is for those claiming that the term satisfies that requirement to show that it does.

Section 3 cannot be evaded by the contract term in question deeming that statements of fact are not representations; *Cremdean Properties Ltd v Nash*, 1977. However, a term which stated that an auctioneer had no authority to make any representation was held to fall outside s.3; *Overbrooke Estates Ltd v Glencombe Properties Ltd*, 1974.

Section 3 of the Misrepresentation Act 1967 does not apply to "consumer contracts" under the Consumer Rights Act; when it has been brought into force, terms purporting to exclude or restrict liability for misrepresentation in such contracts will be subject to the assessment of fairness in Part 2 of the new Act.

Figure 15: Remedies for Misrepresentation

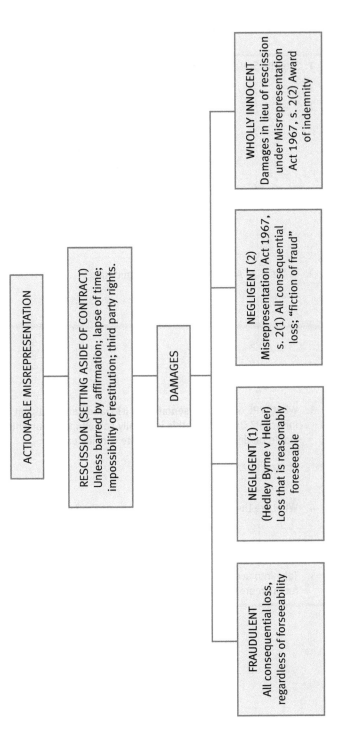

Figure 16: Action Guide to Answering Questions on Misrepresentation

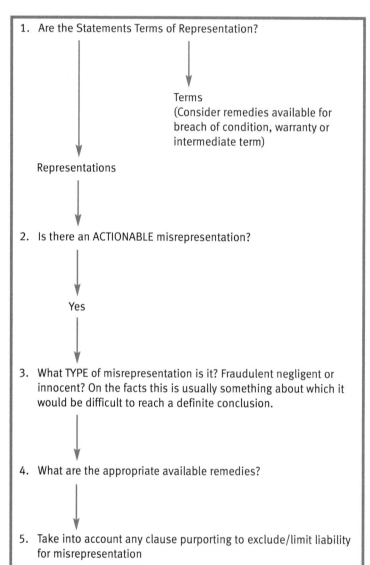

1. Are the Statements Terms of Representation?

    Terms
    (Consider remedies available for breach of condition, warranty or intermediate term)

    Representations

2. Is there an ACTIONABLE misrepresentation?

    Yes

3. What TYPE of misrepresentation is it? Fraudulent negligent or innocent? On the facts this is usually something about which it would be difficult to reach a definite conclusion.

4. What are the appropriate available remedies?

5. Take into account any clause purporting to exclude/limit liability for misrepresentation

You should now know and understand:

- the circumstances in which a contract may be avoided on the grounds of an actionable misrepresentation;
- the differences between fraudulent, negligent and wholly innocent misrepresentation;
- the circumstances in which a contract may be rescinded for misrepresentation;
- the basis upon which damages are awarded for misrepresentation;
- the circumstances in which liability for misrepresentation can be excluded.

QUESTION AND ANSWER

THE QUESTION

Richard owned and ran a shop in Nottingley selling sunbeds. Richard advertised the business and premises for sale in the local paper, stating that under the planning regulations the premises could legally be used as offices.

Nancy saw the advertisement and visited the shop premises. She was told by Richard that the profits of the business were £200,000 per year and that she could expect the figure to rise significantly by 30 per cent in the following year. Richard invited Nancy to examine the accounts but she declined to do so. Had she done so, she would have noticed that the profits were on a downward trend and had never exceeded £70,000 per year.

The day after this conversation, Richard was notified by Nottingley Council that the street on which the premises were situated would be permanently closed to traffic in the near future. Richard did not pass on this information to Nancy.

Four months later, Nancy entered into a written contract to purchase the business and premises which made no reference to the statements referred to above. On taking possession, Nancy discovered that Richard's statement as to the planning position was incorrect as the shop premises could not be used as offices without planning permission. She also discovered the true position as to the profits.

Soon after the purchase, the local authority closed the street and Nancy lost much of the passing trade. Nevertheless, Nancy carried on but after the end of the first year of trading the profits of the business are no longer sufficient to cover its outgoings.

Advise Nancy.

ADVICE AND THE ANSWER

General guidance

A useful way of approaching questions on misrepresentation is to follow the action guide set out in Figure 16 above. As a preliminary issue you may need to consider whether any of the statements made have become terms of the contract. This may be difficult to establish on the facts but the best approach is to apply the criteria set out in Chapter 6 above under the heading "Terms and Representations".

When deciding whether there is an actionable misrepresentation you must analyse the statements very closely. You should bear in mind that there is a very fine line between, e.g., statements of opinion and statements of fact, and be vigilant for statements that are actionable because they amount to a "half-truth" or where there has been a change circumstances since when the statement was made and when it was relied on. You need to try to establish whether statements are fraudulent, negligent or innocent; again, this can be difficult but remember that, under s.2(1) of the Misrepresentation Act 1967, the false statement is assumed to be fraudulent (the "fiction of fraud") and the burden is placed on the maker of the statement to prove that it was wholly innocent, i.e. that they had reasonable grounds for believing in its truth. The burden of proof is therefore reversed.

When considering remedies, you will need to consider whether rescission is available or whether it has been barred by affirmation, lapse of time, third party rights or the impossibility of restitution. The type of misrepresentation (i.e. fraudulent, negligent or wholly innocent) is significant in terms of the damages available. Thus where the misrepresentation is negligent under s.2(1), damages may be awarded on the same basis as fraud.

1 Are the statements terms or representations?
   (a) This depends on the intention of the parties: criteria include the timing of the statement; its importance; special skill or knowledge on the part of the maker of the statement; and whether the contract has been reduced to writing.
   (b) On the facts, the four month interval between between the making of the statement and the entry by Nancy into the contract may be decisive—the statements are representations (*Routledge v McKay*, CA, 1954).

2 Is there any actionable misrepresentation?
   (a) The definition of misrepresentation: a false statement of fact which induces the innocent party to enter the contract.
   (b) Statement as to the use of premises. Is this a statement of law? Traditionally such statements were not actionable; however, in *Kleinwort Benson Ltd v Lincoln City Council*, HL 1998, it was held that mistakes of law could be actionable. This was applied to misrepresentation in *Pankhania v London Borough of Hackney*, 2002.
   (c) Statement as to the profits. The statement as to the current profits is a false statement of fact. What of the statement as to the future profits? It depends upon whether the statement is one of opinion or fact. It is probably the latter owing to knowledge on the part of the maker (*Smith v Land and House Property Corp*, CA, 1884; *Edgington v Fitzmaurice*, CA, 1885).
   (d) Note that the misrepresentation may be an inducement despite the invitation to examine the accounts; *Redgrave v Hurd*, CA, 1881.
   (e) Closure of street. Normally, silence or non-disclosure is not misrepresentation; however, a duty of disclosure may arise where there is a change of circumstances (*With v O'Flanagan*, CA, 1936).

3 Type of misrepresentation
Even if fraud by Richard could be established, Nancy would be advised to bring proceedings under s.2(1) of the Misrepresentation Act 1967 as the burden of proof shifts from Nancy to Richard.

Remedies
   (a) Rescission may be barred on the grounds of affirmation (*Long v Lloyd*, CA, 1958); Nancy must be aware of right to rescind; *Peyman v Lanjani*, CA, 1985.
   (b) Damages under section 2(1) of the Act of 1967 will be assessed

on the same basis as fraud; *Royscot Trust Ltd v Rogerson*, CA, 1991. A claim for loss of profits on the "loss of opportunity" basis is not precluded; *East v Maurer*, CA, 1991.

Mistake

INTRODUCTION

This chapter examines the circumstances in which a contract may be void on the grounds of an operative mistake. This involves a consideration of:

1. The circumstances in which a document entered into as a result of, or containing, a mistake may be invalid
2. The concept of identical or common mistake
3. Non-identical mistake, which is divided into mutual and unilateral mistake
4. The circumstances in which a contract may be void on the grounds of a mistaken identity

In certain circumstances, a contract may be void at common law owing to a mistake made by the parties concerning the contract. The situations in which a contract will be nullified for mistake are contained in a disparate group of cases; there is no underlying general "doctrine" of mistake. A mistake which has the effect of rendering a contract void is described as an "operative" mistake. However, in determining the issue of mistake, there is a threshold question that first has to be considered, i.e. whether the contract itself, expressly or impliedly, provides which party should bear the risk of the mistake; *Kalsep Ltd v X-Flow BV*, 2001.

The scope of operative mistake now extends to mistakes of law as well as fact; *Kleinwort Benson Ltd v Lincoln City Council*, HL, 1999 and *Brennan v Bolt Burden*, CA, 2004. The law relating to mistake will be considered under four headings: mistake relating to documents; identical or "common" mistake; non-identical mistake; and mistake as to identity.

MISTAKE RELATING TO DOCUMENTS

Non est Factum
As a general rule, a person is bound by his or her signature to a document, whether or not they have read or understood the document; *L'Estrange v Graucob*, 1934. Where a person has been induced to sign a contractual document by fraud or misrepresentation, the transaction will be voidable.

Similarly, if one of the other forms of mistake discussed in this chapter are present the contract may be void.

In the absence of such mistake, the plea of non est factum (not my deed) may be available. The plea is an ancient one and was originally used to protect illiterate persons. It eventually became available to literate persons who had signed a document believing it to be something totally different from what it actually was. Thus, in *Foster v Mackinnon*, 1869, the defendant, a senile man with poor eyesight, was induced to sign a document which he was told was a guarantee. In fact, it was a bill of exchange upon which the claimant ultimately became entitled. It was held that the defendant, who had not been negligent, was not liable on the bill; the plea of non est factum succeeded.

An unrestrained right to raise the plea would lead to abuse and uncertainty and so the courts have placed two restrictions on the right to raise the plea,

(i) the signer's mistake as to the nature of the document must be fundamental or radical; and

(ii) the signer must not have been careless in signing the document.

With regard to (i), the courts originally took the view that the plea was not available where the signer's mistake was merely as to the contents of the document rather than as to its character or class; *Howatson v Webb*, CA, 1908. This test was not a realistic one and was substituted by the House of Lords in *Saunders v Anglia Building Society*, HL, 1971. The test is now that there must be a fundamental or radical difference between the document actually signed and what the signer believed it to be.

With regard to (ii), the Court of Appeal had ruled in *Carlisle and Cumberland Banking Co v Bragg*, CA, 1911 that negligence on the part of the signer only defeated the plea if the document was a negotiable instrument. The distinction was illogical and Bragg's case was overruled by Saunders; the position is now that the plea cannot be raised by a signer who has been careless.

KEY CASE

SAUNDERS V ANGLIA BUILDING SOCIETY, HL, 1971

An elderly widow wished to transfer the title of her house to her nephew by way of gift. Her nephew and a man named Lee prepared a document assigning the property to Lee and asked her to sign. She signed it unread as she had lost her spectacles and trusted her nephew. Lee mortgaged the property to the Building Society and disposed of the moneys raised for his own use. He defaulted on the repayments and the Building Society sought possession of the house. Saunders (the widow's executrix) sought a declaration that the assignment to Lee was void by reason of non est factum.

Held: The plea could not be raised because:

(i) the transaction the widow had entered was not fundamentally different from what she intended at the time she entered it; and

(ii) she had been careless in signing the document; she could at least have made sure that the transfer was to the person intended by her.

Comment

The effect of *Saunders v Anglia Building Society* is, if anything, to restrict further the circumstances in which the plea of non est factum can be successfully raised.

Rectification

Where the parties are agreed on the terms of the contract but by mistake record them incorrectly in a subsequent written document, the remedy of rectification may be available. The court can rectify the error and order specific performance of the contract as rectified. The remedy is an exception to the parol evidence rule (see Chapter 6) as oral evidence is admissible to show that the written document is in error. Following *Chartbrook v Persimmon Homes*, it is accepted that (if ascertainable from the background of a contract embodied in a document) where that the parties have made a mistake in the way that they have expressed their agreement, it can be corrected as part of the process of construction rather than by an order of rectification. Such "corrective interpretation" is more likely where the parties have made an error of language, but less likely where a particular provision has been mistakenly omitted. In such a case rectification may lie.

In order to obtain rectification the following must be established:

(1) There must be a concluded antecedent agreement upon which the written document was based. The agreement need not necessarily be a finally binding contract; *Joscelyne v Nissen*, 1970.

(2) The written document must fail to record what the parties had agreed. In *Frederick E. Rose (London) Ltd v William H. Pim Co Ltd*, CA, 1953, the parties had contracted for the sale of a type of horsebean and the written contract referred to "horsebeans". The goods delivered were not of the type the parties had in mind. Rectification was refused since the written contract correctly recorded what the parties had agreed.

(3) The written document must fail to express the common intention of the parties. However, if one party mistakenly believes the document gives effect to that intention and the other party is aware of this mistake but

nevertheless is guilty of sharp practice in allowing the contract to be executed, rectification may be ordered; *A. Roberts Co v Leicestershire CC*, 1961.

(4) It must be equitable to grant the remedy; in particular, it will be refused where third parties have acquired rights on the faith of the written contract.

IDENTICAL OR COMMON MISTAKE

CHECKPOINT

In "identical" or "common" mistake, the parties, although apparently in agreement, have entered into a contract on the basis of a false and fundamental assumption. It may be described as identical or common mistake since both parties make the same error. The contract is not necessarily void at common law in these circumstances. The cases are categorised as set out below.

Mistake as to the Existence of the Subject-matter

The contract will be void at common law if, unknown to the parties, the subject-matter of the agreement does not exist or has ceased to exist. In *Couturier v Hastie*, HL, 1856, a cargo of corn, en route to London, had to be sold at a port of refuge as it had begun to ferment. Unaware of this, the parties agreed a sale of the corn in London. It was held that the seller was not entitled to the price of the cargo. The facts of the case fall into what is now s.6 of the Sale of Goods Act, which provides that where there is a contract for the sale of specific goods and the goods, without the knowledge of the seller have perished at the time when the contract was made, the contract is void.

The transaction may also be void where the parties contract on the basis of a false assumption which underlies it. In *Galloway v Galloway*, 1914, a man and woman, believing they were lawfully married, entered into a separation deed. In fact the "marriage" was invalid and therefore the separation agreement was likewise void.

It may be, however, that the proper construction of the contract is that the risk of the subject-matter or state of affairs not being in existence falls on one party or the other. For example, one party may be warranting the existence of the subject-matter; if so, the contract is valid; *McRae v Commonwealth Disposals Commission*, 1950. The remedy will lie in an award of damages.

Mistake as to Title

The contract will be void at common law in the (rare) situation where one party agrees to transfer property to the other which the latter already owns and neither party is aware of the fact. In *Cooper v Phibbs*, HL, 1867, the House of Lords set aside an agreement whereby A had agreed to lease a fishery to B, but unknown to either, the fishery was already owned by B.

Mistake as to Quality

There is some authority that an identical mistake as to the quality of the subject-matter may not be operative at common law. Thus, if A sells to B a painting which both parties mistakenly believe to have been painted by Constable, and therefore valuable, but in fact which is not by Constable and is worth far less, the contract is valid (in the absence of actionable misrepresentation or assumption of risk by either party); *Leaf v International Galleries*, CA, 1950. The leading case is discussed below.

KEY CASE

BELL v LEVER BROS LTD, HL, 1932

Bell, an employee of Lever, entered into an agreement to terminate his employment under which he was paid £30,000 compensation. It was later discovered that Bell could have been dismissed without compensation due to certain breaches of contract by him and about which he had forgotten. The House of Lords was prepared to treat the situation as one of common mistake as to quality.

Held: The contract was valid. Lord Atkin said that mistake as to the quality of the thing contracted for will not affect consent unless it is a mistake of both parties, and is as to the existence "of some quality which makes the thing without the quality essentially different from the thing it was believed to be".

Comment

As the mistake in *Bell v Lever Bros* was in some sense fundamental, the case has been interpreted as deciding that an identical mistake as to quality can never render the contract void at common law.

Subsequent decisions tend to support the view stated in the comment above; for example, *Leaf v International Galleries* and *Harrison and Jones Ltd v Bunten and Lancaster Ltd*, 1953. Nevertheless, there are dicta in the speeches of the House of Lords in *Bell v Lever Bros* which suggest that a contract may be void if the mistake as to quality is sufficiently fundamental, and support for this view is to be found in the cases of *Associated Japanese*

Bank Ltd v Credit du Nord, 1988 and *Great Peace Shipping Ltd v Tsavliris (Salvage) International Ltd*, CA, 2002.

In the latter case the ship Great Providence was damaged and in danger of sinking. The owners engaged the defendants to recover her, and the defendants were informed by a third party that the claimants' ship Great Peace was in close proximity. The defendants accordingly hired the Great Peace for a minimum of five days to assist in her recovery. The claimants sought to recover the hire. Toulson J held that the contract was not void at common law as the mistake was not sufficiently fundamental; the Great Peace was not so far away as to be incapable of providing the service required. Thus, the risk fell on the defendants. This decision was subsequently affirmed by the Court of Appeal which held that the mistake as to the distance between the two vessels was not such as to render the services supplied by the claimants "essentially different" from what the parties had agreed. However, the court considered that a common mistake as to quality could render a contract void if it satisfied the "essential difference" test in *Bell v Lever Bros*.

Identical or Common Mistake in Equity

Until quite recently, it was accepted that where there was a common mistake as to quality, although the agreement was valid at law, it was apparently voidable in equity. Thus, in *Solle v Butcher*, CA, 1950, the claimant agreed to lease a flat from the defendant, both parties mistakenly believing that the premises were not subject to rent-control. The Court of Appeal held that the mistake was not such as would render the lease void at law, but the court would set aside the contract in equity. To do justice, terms were imposed that the claimant should either give up the flat or stay on at the maximum rent chargeable by law.

Similar examples of rescission in equity of contracts entered into under an identical mistake as to quality were *Grist v Bailey*, 1967 (sale of a house) and *Magee v Pennine Insurance Co Ltd*, CA, 1969 (contract of insurance). However, these authorities require re-appraisal as a result of the *Great Peace Shipping* case (discussed above) where Toulson J controversially doubted the very existence of the doctrine of rescission in equity of a contract on the grounds of common mistake. The judge was "at a loss as to what is the test for determining the nature of the 'fundamental mistake' necessary to give birth to the right to rescind". This approach was affirmed by the Court of Appeal who held that there is no jurisdiction to grant rescission of a contract on the ground of common mistake where that contract is valid and enforceable on common law grounds. Thus, the court disapproved *Solle v Butcher* on the basis that it was not good law.

NON-IDENTICAL MISTAKE

CHECKPOINT

In non-identical mistake, the parties do not both make the same mistake. A non-identical mistake is said to be "mutual" where the parties misunderstand each other's intentions and are at cross-purposes; and "unilateral" where only one party is mistaken and the other party is aware of the mistake.

Mutual Mistake

Operative mutual mistake is illustrated by *Raffles v Wichelhaus*, 1864. The defendants agreed to buy cotton from the claimants ex the ship Peerless from Bombay. Two ships of that name were due to leave Bombay; the defendants had in mind the ship leaving in October and the claimants had in mind the ship leaving in December. The court held that the transaction was too ambiguous to be enforced as a contract.

The test applied by the court in this type of case is to consider whether a reasonable third party would take the agreement to mean what one party, A, understood it to mean or what the other party, B, understood it to mean. It is only when the transaction is totally ambiguous under this objective test that the contract is void. Thus, in *Wood v Scarth*, 1858, the defendant offered in writing to let a pub to the claimant at £63 per year. After a conversation with the defendant's clerk, the claimant accepted by letter, believing that the £63 rental was the only payment under the contract. The defendant had intended that a £500 premium would also be payable and he believed that his clerk had explained this to the claimant. It was held that the contract as understood by the claimant would be enforced and the court awarded him damages.

By comparison, in *Scriven v Hindley*, 1913, at an auction, the defendants' bid for a lot consisting of tow was accepted. The defendants believed that they had bid for hemp. Their bid was right for hemp but extravagant for tow, although the auctioneer was unaware of the true nature of the defendants' mistake. However, the catalogue and samples were misleadingly described and marked, and these factors, together with other circumstances, meant that the reasonable person could not say whether the contract was for hemp or tow. The contract was held to be void.

If the contract is void at common law on the ground of a mutual mistake, equity "follows the law" and an order of specific performance will be refused. However, even where the contract is valid at law, specific performance will be refused if to grant it would cause hardship.

MISTAKE

Unilateral Mistake

Here one party is fundamentally mistaken concerning the contract and the other party is aware of the mistake, or the circumstances are such that he may be taken to be aware of it.

For a unilateral mistake to be operative, the mistake by one party must be as to the terms of the contract itself, as in *Hartog v Colin and Shields*, 1939. Here the defendants offered goods to the claimant at a certain price per pound but had intended to offer them at the same price per piece. The value of a piece was one third that of a pound. It was held that the circumstances were such that the claimants must have realised the defendant's error, which, as it concerned a term of the contract, rendered the contract void.

A mere error of judgment as to some fact such as the quality of the subject-matter will not suffice to render the contract void for unilateral mistake.

KEY CASE

SMITH V HUGHES, 1871
The defendant was shown a sample of new oats by the claimant. The defendant bought them in the belief that they were "old" oats; he did not want "new" oats. Was the contract void for mistake?

Held: The mistake was merely as to the quality of the subject-matter and could not render the contract void, even if the claimant seller knew of the mistake.

Comment
The rule established by *Smith v Hughes* was followed in *Statoil v Louis Dreyfus Energy Services LP*, 2008, the judge stating that the correctness of the long-standing rule "has never been doubted".

In *Daventry DC v Daventry and District Housing Ltd*, CA, 2011, the court affirmed that (in the context of the rectification of a document) that the test for an operative unilateral mistake has four elements:

1. One party (A) must be mistaken about the inclusion or omission of a particular term in the document;
2. the other party (B) must be aware of the omission or exclusion and that it was due to A's mistake;
3. B has omitted to tell A of the mistake; and
4. the mistake must be calculated to benefit B.

As with mutual mistake, equity follows the law and will refuse specific performance of a contract affected by unilateral mistake as in *Webster v Cecil*,

1861. In that case, the defendant, who had already refused to sell his property to the plaintiff for £2,000, wrote offering to sell it to him for £1,250. This offer was immediately accepted. The defendant had intended to write £2,250. It was held that the mistake was operative and specific performance would be refused.

Figure 17: Operative Mistake

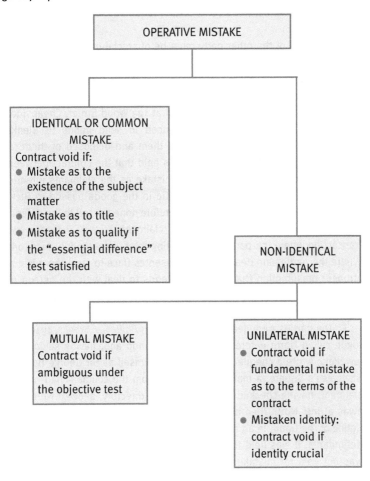

. . . .

MISTAKE AS TO IDENTITY

Where one party is mistaken as to the identity of the other party, in certain circumstances the contract may be void at common law.

Almost all the decided cases of operative mistake in this area are in fact instances of unilateral mistake, as the non-mistaken party is aware of the mistake because they have engineered it through their own fraud. Even where the contract is not void, it may be voidable for fraudulent misrepresentation and if the goods which are the subject-matter have passed to an innocent third party before the contract is avoided, that third party may acquire a good title (see below for examples).

For the contract to be void, certain requirements must be satisfied:

1. The identity of the other party must be of crucial importance.

In *Cundy v Lindsay*, HL, 1878, the claimants received an order for linen from a rogue, Blenkarn, who gave his address as 37 Wood Street, Cheapside. In the correspondence, he imitated the signature of a reputable firm, Blenkiron and Co, known to the claimants, who traded at 123 Wood Street, Cheapside. The claimants were thus fraudulently induced to send goods to Blenkarn's address, where he took possession of them and disposed of them to the defendants, innocent purchasers. It was held that the contract between the claimants and Blenkarn was void for mistake as the claimants intended to deal only with Blenkiron and Co. No title in the goods passed to Blenkarn (because the contract was void) and therefore none passed to the defendants who were liable in conversion to the claimants. *Cundy v Lindsay* was a transaction where the parties were dealing inter absentes (not face-to-face). Where the parties are dealing inter praesentes (face-to-face) there is a much stronger presumption that a person intends to deal with the person physically before them. Thus any mistake is likely to be as to that person's attributes (e.g. their creditworthiness) rather than their identity.

The parties were dealing face-to-face in *Phillips v Brooks*, 1919. Here, a rogue called North entered the claimant's shop and, having selected some jewellery, wrote a cheque and announced himself as Sir George Bullough of St. James's Square, a man of means of whom the claimant had heard. The claimant, having checked this address in a directory, allowed North to take away a ring. North then pledged the ring with the defendants, who had no notice of the fraud. In an action by the claimants to recover the ring from the defendants, it was held that the contract between the claimants and North was not void for mistake, because the claimants had intended to contract with the person in the shop, whoever it was. The only mistake was as to the customer's credit-worthiness, not his identity. The contract was, however, voidable for fraud but because the defendants had acquired the ring in good faith before the contract was sought to be set aside, they acquired a good title.

Despite *Phillips v Brooks*, identity was held to be crucial in *Ingram v Little*, CA, 1961. The claimants, elderly women, advertised their car for sale. A rogue, calling himself P. G. M. Hutchinson of an address in Caterham, offered to buy it. The claimants would only accept a cheque when they had checked, from a directory, that there was such a person at that address. The cheque was worthless and the rogue disposed of the car to the defendant, who took in good faith. It was held that the contract between the claimants and the rogue was void for mistake. The decision in this case is very difficult to distinguish from *Phillips v Brooks* and was doubted by the House of Lords in *Shogun Finance Ltd v Norman Hudson*, HL, 2002 (discussed below).

The decision in *Phillips v Brooks* was followed by Court of Appeal in the case below.

KEY CASE

Lewis v Averay, CA, 1972
The claimant, a postgraduate student, advertised a car for sale and was visited by a rogue posing as the actor Richard Greene, who offered to buy it. The rogue signed a cheque but the claimant only allowed him to take the car away after being shown a forged studio admission pass. The cheque was worthless and the rogue sold the car to the defendant, an innocent purchaser.

Held: The contract, though voidable for fraud, was not void. The court took the view that, where the parties are face-to-face, there is a very strong presumption that a person intends to deal with the person before him, as identified by sight and hearing.

Comment
In effect, the court adopted an objective approach and did not attempt to identify the claimant's intention.

A mistake as to identity should be distinguished from a mistake as to the capacity in which a party deals. Thus, in *Hardman v Booth*, 1863, the claimants, intending to sell cloth to Thomas Gandell Co, negotiated with one Edward Gandell at the firm's offices. Edward, an employee and not a member of the firm, intended to take possession of the goods for his own use. Having obtained possession, he sold them to the defendant, an innocent third party. It was held that the contract between the claimants and Edward was void. The claimants had believed he was a representative of the firm and never intended to deal with him personally.

It is sometimes stated that an additional requirement for the contract to be void is that the mistaken party must have taken reasonable steps to verify the identity of the other party. It may be that this is more in the nature of an evidential burden to establish that the identity of the other party is crucial.

2. The mistaken party must have in mind an identifiable person with whom they intend to contract.

This requirement was not satisfied in *King's Norton Metal Co v Edridge Merrett Co Ltd*, CA, 1897. The claimants received a letter purporting to be from "Hallam & Co" with an impressive letterhead. In fact Hallam was a fictitious firm consisting entirely of a rogue named Wallis. The claimants despatched goods on credit to the bogus company. The court took the view that the claimants had intended to contract with the writer of the letter, whoever it may be, and the contract was not void for mistake. The only mistake was as to the credit-worthiness of the other party and not as to his identity. This decision should be compared with *Cundy v Lindsay* (above).

3. The other party must be aware of the mistake.

In the cases discussed above, identity was fraudulently misrepresented and therefore the requirement was satisfied. An unusual case in this context is *Boulton v Jones*, 1857. The claimant was employed by Brocklehurst, a pipe hose manufacturer, with whom the defendants had had previous dealings. The claimant took over Brocklehurst's business and on the same day the defendants ordered hose from Brocklehurst. The claimant supplied the goods but the defendants refused to pay on the ground that they intended to contract, not with the claimant, but with Brocklehurst as they wished to enforce a set-off against him. It was held that there was no contract, although the precise state of knowledge of the claimant was not made clear. If the claimant was unaware of the fact that the offer was not intended for him then, arguably, the contract was valid.

The position with regard to contracts made in writing was considered in the case below.

KEY CASE

SHOGUN FINANCE LTD V NORMAN HUDSON, HL, 2002

A rogue, X, went to a dealer to buy a car on hire purchase. X produced the stolen driving licence of P and the dealer checked these details with the claimant finance company, which approved the transaction. X then sold the vehicle to an innocent purchaser. The claimant finance company argued that the agreement with X was void because they intended only to contract with P and the identity of P was a matter of vital importance. The Court of Appeal held that H did not obtain a good title; i.e. the hire purchase contract was void. H appealed to the House of Lords.

Held: The decision was upheld. The finance company was only willing to do business with the person identified in the written agreement and no one else.

Comment
The face to face principle has no application to a case where the contract is wholly in writing. In such cases the identity of the vendor and purchaser is established by the names of the parties included in the written contract.

In arriving at the above decision, their Lordships held that H had not acquired good title under s.27 of the Hire Purchase Act 1964. Under that provision, a private purchaser, acting in good faith without notice of the hire purchase agreement, who buys a car from a seller (a "debtor") who in turn holds the car under a hire purchase agreement, will obtain a good title. However, it was held that the debtor under the hire purchase agreement was P, not the rogue, and so the 1964 act did not apply.

Figure 18: Mistaken Identity

REVISION CHECKLIST

You should now know and understand:

- ☐ the circumstances in which a written document may be void on the grounds of non est factum;
- ☐ when a written contract may be rectified;
- ☐ the circumstances in which a contract may be void on the grounds of a common mistake;
- ☐ when a contract may be void for mutual or unilateral mistake;
- ☐ the circumstances in which a contract may be void on the grounds of a mistaken identity.

QUESTION AND ANSWER

THE QUESTION

George owned a painting which he believed to be a reproduction of a work by John Singer Sargent, the famous American water-colourist. He sold the painting to Harry, who also believed it to be a reproduction, for £80.

Harry, having consulted an expert after acquiring the painting, discovered that the painting was a genuine original work by Sargent. Harry intended to sell it to a London dealer, Ian. After a telephone conversation with Ian concerning the merits of the painting, Harry sent it to him with a letter offering to sell it. Unfortunately, the price quoted in the letter was £80 instead of £800 (the true value of the picture). Harry's secretary had inadvertently omitted a nought. Ian sent Harry a cheque for £80 and now refuses to return the painting to him.

George, having now discovered that the painting is genuine, wishes to recover it.

Discuss the legal position of the parties.

General guidance

Before attempting any question on mistake, it will be necessary to have a good understanding of the distinction between the three categories of mistake: common, mutual and unilateral. It is important to grasp that the circumstances in which a contract may be vitiated by mistake have been very narrowly circumscribed by the courts—the maxim "caveat emptor" prevails. There is also a very close interrelationship with the law of misrepresentation, particularly where mistakes as to identity are concerned. Where the contract in such cases is not void for mistake, it is likely to be voidable on the grounds of fraudulent misrepresentation. It follows that even where there is no operative mistake, there may be actionable misrepresentation; a good illustration of this possibility is the case of *Leaf v International Galleries*, CA, 1950. However, in that case, the right to rescind for misrepresentation had been lost through the lapse of time.

Answer plan

1 George's only chance of recovering the painting would depend upon showing that the contract between himself and Harry is void for mistake. Although a contract may be void for a common mistake where the mistake relates to the existence of the subject-matter or some fundamental fact underlying the contract, where the mistake relates to the quality of the subject-matter, there is authority that the contract is valid; *Bell v Lever Bros Ltd*, HL, 1932.

2 In that case, Lord Atkin said, obiter, that if A buys a picture from B and both A and B believe the work to be that of an old master and a high price is paid, if it turns out to be a modern copy, A has no remedy, in the absence of representation or warranty. This dictum was effectively followed in *Leaf v International Galleries*, CA, 1950 where the court refused to hold void a contract for the sale of a picture where both buyer and seller mistakenly believed it had been painted by John Constable.

3 Despite these authorities, it might be worth arguing that the parties have contracted for something essentially different from what they believed and therefore the contract is void. In *Bell v Lever Bros Ltd*, Lord Atkin also said that the contract may be void where the mistake is as to the existence of some quality which renders the thing without the quality "essentially different from the thing it was believed to be". A dictum of Steyn J in *Associated Japanese Bank Ltd v Credit du Nord*, 1988 and of Lord Phillips on *Great Peace Shipping Ltd v Tsavliris*

(Salvage) International Ltd, CA, 2003 support the view that a mistake as to quality could be operative in such circumstances.

4 Some authority for such an argument may be found in *Nicholson and Venn v Smith Marriott*, 1947, where the defendants put up for auction table napkins described as having belonged to Charles I. On the faith of this description, the claimant bought them but they turned out to be Georgian and worth much less than the claimant paid for them. The buyer recovered damages for breach of contract but Hallet J said, obiter, that the contract could have been treated as void for mistake.

5 In an American case, *Sherwood v Walker*, 1887, the defendants sold the plaintiffs a cow. It was accepted by the majority of the court that both parties believed her to be barren but in fact she was in calf and worth about 10 times what the plaintiffs paid for her. The contract was held invalid on the ground that the mistake was not merely as to the quality of the animal, but as to the very nature of the thing.

6 In the absence of operative mistake, George might be able to recover damages if Harry had warranted or represented that the painting was a Sargent. Rescission for misrepresentation here could only be ordered if the contract between Harry and Ian is also void. This is discussed below.

7 Turning to the contract between Harry and Ian, Harry may be able to obtain an order of rescission in equity on the ground of operative unilateral mistake. A contract will be void for unilateral mistake where the mistake is as to the terms of the contract and the other party is, or must be taken to be, aware of the mistake; *Hartog v Colin and Shields*, 1939. Here, because of the prior telephone call, it is likely that Ian is well aware of the true value of the painting and therefore must be taken to know that the sum stated in the offer is a mistake.

8 In *Webster v Cecil*, 1861, the parties were negotiating the sale of some property and the vendor wrote to the purchaser offering £1,250 instead of £2,250. It was held that since the vendor had already refused to sell for £2,000, the purchaser must have been aware of the mistake and specific performance was refused.

Duress and Undue Influence

10

INTRODUCTION

This chapter addresses the concepts of duress and undue influence. This involves a consideration of:

1   The circumstances in which a contract may be avoided on the grounds of duress
2   The circumstances in which a contract may be avoided for undue influence
3   Undue influence and third parties

The agreement may be the result of some improper pressure exerted by one party over the other. The problem is dealt with by the common law doctrine of duress and the equitable doctrine of undue influence.

DURESS

Duress is a common law concept under which a contract may be avoided. It seems that duress renders a contract voidable; *Pao On v Lau Yiu Long*, PC, 1980.

The scope of duress at common law was very narrow and confined to unlawful physical violence to the person or constraint of the other party (actual or threatened); *Cumming v Ince*, 1847. In particular, the early cases refused to recognise "duress of goods" as invalidating a contract. However, modern cases indicate a more flexible approach; in *The Siboen and the Sibotre*, 1976, it was said that a person coerced into a contract by the threat of having his house burnt down or a picture slashed could plead duress.

Based on *Pao On* and other cases, the courts have evolved a doctrine of "economic duress". In *North Ocean Shipping Co Ltd v Hyundai Construction Co Ltd*, 1978, a contract was made to build a supertanker for an agreed price. The seller then refused to complete unless the buyer promised to pay a further 10 per cent. The buyer agreed and made the payments as the ship was needed to fulfil a charter. It was held that the extra payment could in principle be recovered on the ground of economic duress although on the facts of the case it was held that the buyer had affirmed the contract because he had complained too late.

A good illustration of economic duress is provided by the key case below.

KEY CASE

ATLAS EXPRESS LTD V KAFCO, 1989.
The defendants were contracted to supply basketware to branches of Woolworths and entered into a contract with the claimants to deliver the baskets at an agreed price. In error, the claimants set the price too low and then refused to deliver the goods unless the defendants paid a higher price. Fearing that they would be unable to find another carrier, and that the breach of contract would be ruinous, the defendants under protest paid the extra sum.

Held: The agreement was vitiated by duress. The defendants had no real alternative—they felt they were "over a barrel".

Comment
In this case, the threat to break the contract was explicit and direct. In other cases an indirect "veiled" threat has been held to amount to duress, as in *B & S Contracts and Design Ltd v Victor Green Publications Ltd*, 1984.

In *DSND Subsea Ltd v Petroleum Geo-Services ASA*, 2000 Dyson J set out the factors that must be established in order to sustain a claim of economic duress:

"The ingredients of actionable duress are that there must be pressure, (a) whose practical effect is that there is compulsion on, or a lack of practical choice for, the victim; (b) which is illegitimate; and (c) which is a significant cause inducing the claimant to enter into the contract. In determining whether there has been illegitimate pressure, the court takes into account a range of factors. These include whether there has been an actual or threatened breach of contract; whether the person allegedly exerting the pressure has acted in good or bad faith; whether the victim had any realistic alternative but to submit to the pressure; whether the victim protested at the time; and whether he affirmed and sought to rely on the contract ... [i]llegitimate pressure must be distinguished from the rough and tumble of the pressures of normal commercial bargaining."

In *Pao On v Lau Yiu Long*, Lord Scarman considered that "coercion of the will" was the essence of duress. However, in recent years this theory has fallen out of favour and later cases have stressed the test of causation. In *Dimskal Shipping Co SA v International Transport Workers Federation*, HL, 1992, Lord Goff stated that the economic pressure must constitute "a significant cause inducing [the claimant] to enter the relevant contract". In *CTN Cash and Carry v Gallagher*, CA, 1994, it was suggested that, in appropriate circumstances, a threat to commit a lawful act could amount to duress. This represents a potentially difficult extension of the doctrine. In *Progress Bulk Carriers Ltd v Tube City IMC LCC*, 2012, it was held that "illegitimate pressure" for the purposes of duress could consist of conduct which was not in itself unlawful, although it would be an unusual case where this was so, particularly in the commercial context.

UNDUE INFLUENCE

The narrow scope of the common law doctrine of duress led to the development, in equity, of the doctrine of undue influence.

> **CHECKPOINT**
>
> The doctrine of undue influence applies wherever improper pressure (not amounting to duress at common law) is brought to bear on a party to enter a contract. Where undue influence is found, the contract is voidable; gifts, as well as contracts, may be avoided under the doctrine.

A typical example of the type of case traditionally categorised as undue influence is *Williams v Bayley*, HL, 1866, where a payment of money obtained by a threat to prosecute a close relative for an admitted offence was held to amount to undue influence. It should be noted here that the threat was not in itself unlawful. The modern law has been shaped by two House of Lords' decisions, *Barclays Bank Plc v O'Brien*, HL, 1994 and *Royal Bank of Scotland Plc v Etridge (No.2)*, HL, 2002. As a result of these cases, undue influence may be categorised as follows:

1 Actual undue influence. The claimant must establish that the defendant used undue influence in relation to particular transaction. There does not need to be any previous history of such influence, although there is normally some relationship between the parties, such as husband and wife: *Bank of Credit and Commerce SA v Aboody*, CA, 1990. In *CIBC Mortgages Plc v Pitt*, HL,

1993, it was held that the transaction does not have to be to the victim's manifest disadvantage before the court will exercise its power to rescind.

2 (a) Special relationship. This category applies to certain established special "fiduciary" relationships: parent and child; guardian and ward; religious advisor and disciple; solicitor and client; and trustee and beneficiary (but not husband and wife). Such a special relationship gives rise to a presumption of influence only, but not undue influence. If the transaction in question is suspicious, i.e. it "calls for an explanation", then a second evidential presumption, of undue influence, will arise. This second presumption, unlike the first, is rebuttable.

(b) No special relationship. This category covers cases where there is no special relationship as explained above, but the relationship is nevertheless one of "trust and confidence" where one party is in a position to exert undue influence over the other. Following *Etridge* there is no longer any presumption of undue influence in such cases. The claimant must show they placed trust and confidence in the defendant; once that is established, then, where there is a transaction "calling for an explanation" an evidential presumption that there has been undue influence will arise. It will be for the defendant to prove that no such influence was exercised.

Thus, an inference of undue influence may also apply even if the relationship is not within one of the special relationships but one party, by reason of the confidence reposed in him or her by the other weaker party, is able to take unfair advantage. For example, in *Lloyds Bank Ltd v Bundy*, CA, 1975, an elderly farmer gave the Bank a guarantee in respect of his son's overdraft and mortgaged the farmhouse to the Bank as security. It was clear that the farmer had placed himself entirely in the hands of the assistant bank manager and had been given no opportunity to seek independent advice. Although, normally, the presumption of undue influence would not apply between bank and customer, the Court of Appeal held that it did so here and the transaction was set aside.

It was later held by the House of Lords in *National Westminster Bank Plc v Morgan*, HL, 1985 that the transaction would only be avoided in such cases where the transaction itself was "manifestly disadvantageous" to the weaker party. However in the *Etridge* case their Lordships considered that the label "manifest disadvantage" should be abandoned in favour of a test of whether the transaction "calls for an explanation", thus adopting the dictum of Lindley J in *Allcard v Skinner*, 1887: i.e. is the transaction such as "not to be reasonably accounted for on the ground of friendship, relationship, charity or other ordinary motives on which ordinary men act?"

The evidential presumption of undue influence may be rebutted by the beneficiary of the transaction showing that the other party exercised independent free will. This is normally done by proving that the other party received competent independent advice. However, in the *Etridge* case, the House of Lords indicated that the existence of independent advice may not be conclusive.

In *Lloyds Bank v Bundy*, Lord Denning MR had sought to establish a doctrine whereby all the instances where the courts intervene to set aside unconscionable transactions are based on a single unifying principle, namely, "inequality of bargaining power". In *National Westminster Bank v Morgan*, the House of Lords refused to accept such a wide principle. Lord Scarman said, "[T]here is no precisely defined law setting limits to the equitable jurisdiction of a court to relieve against undue influence."

UNDUE INFLUENCE AND THIRD PARTIES

In *Barclays Bank Plc v O'Brien*, HL, 1993, the House of Lords sought to lay down authoritative guidance on the question of undue influence, misrepresentation or other legal wrong exercised by a third party. Their Lordships based their approach on the doctrine of notice. The facts of the case were that a husband misrepresented to his wife the amount of a loan sought from the creditor bank. The wife guaranteed the loan. The transaction was set aside, the House of Lords holding that the bank, being aware that the parties were husband and wife, was put on notice of the possibility of legal wrong. However, the bank had failed to inform the wife of the risks involved and had not advised her to seek independent advice.

Lord Browne-Wilkinson summarised the position as follows:

"Where one cohabitee has entered into an obligation to stand as surety [i.e. guarantor] for the debts of the other cohabitee and the creditor is aware that they are cohabitees:

(1) the surety obligation will be valid and enforceable by the creditor unless the suretyship was procured by the undue influence, misrepresentation or other legal wrong of the principal debtor;

(2) if there has been undue influence, misrepresentation or other legal wrong by the principal debtor, unless the creditor has taken reasonable steps to satisfy himself that the surety entered into the obligation freely and in knowledge of the true facts, the creditor will be unable to enforce the surety obligation because he will be fixed with

constructive notice of the surety's right to set aside the transaction;

(3) unless there are special exceptional circumstances, a creditor will have taken such reasonable steps to avoid being fixed with constructive notice if the creditor warns the surety (at a meeting not attended by the principal debtor) of the amount of her [or his] potential liability and of the risks involved and advises the surety to take independent legal advice."

The above procedures were subject to interpretation in later cases. In *Massey v Midland Bank Plc*, CA, 1995, the Court of Appeal considered that the guidance requirements in O'Brien should not be applied mechanically. A similar approach was taken in *Banco Exterior Internacional v Mann*, CA, 1995. However, in *Credit Lyonnais Bank Nederland v Burch*, CA, 1997, the court considered that the circumstances of the particular relationship (employer/ employee) required strict compliance with the O'Brien guidelines. These apparently conflicting approaches caused much uncertainty.

KEY CASE

ROYAL BANK OF SCOTLAND PLC V ETRIDGE (No.2), HL, 2001
An attempt at reconciliation of the case law and further refinement of the O'Brien principles was made by the House of Lords. The House made it clear that the bank would be put on inquiry whenever the relationship between the surety and the debtor is "non-commercial". However, the suggestion in O'Brien that the bank should have a private meeting with the wife to explain the transaction was not followed in *Etridge*.

The content of the independent legal advice the solicitor advising the wife should give was set out. The solicitor should obtain from the bank any relevant information needed to give the advice. It is not necessary that the solicitor should act only for the wife. He or she should consider whether there are any conflicts of duty or interest and what are the best interests of the wife. The solicitor is not the bank's agent and in the normal case the bank is entitled to proceed on the assumption that the solicitor has done the job properly.

> **Comment**
>
> It remains to be seen whether *Etridge* has struck the right balance. In fact, the *Etridge* solution is to shift the burden from the bank to the solicitor advising the wife—the balance has therefore been struck in the creditor's favour.

BARS TO RELIEF

Where a contract is voidable for duress or undue influence, relief (i.e. rescission) may be barred by:

(i)   affirmation of the contract by the weaker party after the undue pressure or presumptive relationship has terminated;

(ii) lapse of time;

(iii) the impossibility of restitution; and

(iv) the intervention of third party rights. Damages as such are not awarded.

Figure 19: Undue influence and third parties

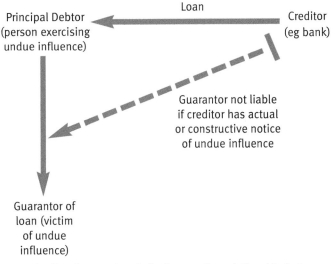

NB: Creditor "put on inquiry" wherever the relationship between principal debtor and guarantor is non-commercial.

REVISION CHECKLIST

You should now know and understand:

☐ the concept of duress as traditionally defined and economic duress; and their effect on a contract;

☐ the circumstances in which a contract will be avoided for undue influence;

☐ the effect of undue influence on the position of third parties.

· ·

QUESTION AND ANSWER
· ·

THE QUESTION

Define and explain what is meant by "duress" and examine critically the development of the doctrine over the last 30 years.

ADVICE AND THE ANSWER

General guidance

Both duress and undue influence are areas where the law has developed considerably in recent times. You can expect examination questions to concentrate on the areas where the law has changed and expanded. With regard to duress, the main development has been in the area of "economic" duress; in the case of undue influence, the courts have grappled with the problems of husband and wife surety cases where the family home is put up as security for a loan. The above problem deals with developments in duress. You should not attempt such a question unless you have a good grasp of the relevant case law. The following Answer plan gives an indication of the scope of the answer.

Answer plan

1 Duress is a concept under which contracts (and gifts) may be avoided. It is generally said to render a contract voidable. The answer should begin with an analysis of the traditional doctrine of duress. Duress was originally very narrowly confined to actual or threatened physical violence to, or unlawful constraint of, the person of the other contracting party—"duress to the person".

2 The doctrine was later extended to "duress of goods", as confirmed in *The Siboen and the Sibotre*, 1976. It seems that, in the case of duress to the person, the threats need not be the only or main reason why the innocent party entered the contract; *Barton v Armstrong*, PC, 1976 (death threats—it made no difference that the contract was in the victim's commercial interests, the contract was still set aside).

3 Since the late 1970s, the courts have been prepared to extend the doctrine to "economic" duress—this may be said to occur where a party is subject to improper economic pressure such that, in entering the contract they cannot be said to have done so freely.

4 Typically this occurs where there is a threat to break an existing contract (an unlawful act) unless the other party renegotiates it on terms favourable to the party issuing the threat; *North Ocean Shipping Co Ltd v Hyundai Construction Co Ltd*, 1978; and *Atlas Express Ltd v Kafco*, 1989.

5 In another group of cases, there is a threat by the defendant to induce a third party to breach a contract with the defendant—this often arises in the context of industrial disputes; *The Universe Sentinel*, HL, 1983.

6 The test for duress—early cases on economic duress were based on the theory of the "overborne will", i.e. the victim, in entering the contract was acting involuntarily (as per Lord Scarman in *Pao On v Lau Yiu Long*, PC, 1980). Latterly it has come to be recognized that in cases of duress, the victim does exercise a choice—it is between the least worst of two undesirable alternatives.

7 Under this approach, the courts are concerned with two matters:
   (i)   the illegitimacy of the threat; and
   (ii) whether the threat amounts to a significant cause in inducing the threatened party to enter the contract, i.e. "causation".

8 With regard to illegitimacy, some cases stress the requirement of "bad faith" (eg *DSND Subsea Ltd v Petroleum Geo-Services ASA*, 2000). Others express doubts as to the necessity for it; e.g. in *Huyton S. A. v Peter Cremer GmbH Ltd*, 1999.

9 Once established that illegitimate pressure has been brought to bear on the victim, it must be shown that the pressure actually caused them to enter the contract. It seems that this may involve showing that the victim had no reasonable alternative to making the contract that they did. In establishing this it will be relevant to consider whether the innocent party:
   (a) did or did not protest;
   (b) whether at the time they had an alternative course such as an adequate legal remedy;

(c)   whether they were independently advised; and

(d)   whether after entering the contract they took steps to avoid it.

10 There is a distinction between actionable duress and "mere commercial pressure"—the latter is not actionable; *Alec Lobb (Garages) Ltd v Total Oil Ltd*, CA, 1985.

11 Lawful act duress—in *CTN Cash and Carry v Gallagher*, CA, 1994 it was suggested that, in appropriate circumstances, a threat to commit a lawful act may be actionable—"lawful act duress". However, it may be necessary to show that the threat was made in circumstances of bad faith; and it is generally accepted that lawful act duress would be rare in a purely commercial context.

12 Support for the notion that duress may arise from a lawful act also comes from a Privy Council decision; *R. v A-G for England and Wales*, PC, 2003.

Illegal and Void Contracts

. . . .

INTRODUCTION

In this chapter we consider the circumstances in which contracts will be held to be illegal and also those contracts which are void either at common law or under statute. This involves an examination of contracts which are:

1. Illegal by statute
2. Illegal on the grounds that they are contrary to public policy
3. Void by statute and at common law
4. Void as being an unreasonable restraint of trade

In *Parkingeye v Somerfield Stores Ltd*, CA, 2012 Sir Robin Jacob observed that "illegality and the law of contract is notoriously knotty territory".

> **CHECKPOINT**
>
> Illegal contracts—as a general proposition, the courts will not enforce contracts of which the purpose is illegal; this includes not only agreements that are criminal in intent but those that are regarded as injurious to society in the wider sense. In addition, there is a distinction between contracts which are actually illegal and those which are void, which is discussed below.

. . . .

ILLEGAL CONTRACTS

Contracts Illegal by Statute

A contract may be expressly forbidden by a statutory provision. For example, in *Re Mahmoud and Ispahani*, CA, 1921, by delegated legislation it was forbidden to buy or sell linseed without first obtaining a licence. The defendant buyer fraudulently stated that he possessed a licence but was held not liable in an action for non-delivery by the innocent seller. The contract was expressly forbidden.

The prohibition may be implied as in *Cope v Rowlands*, 1836, where a statute required that persons acting as stockbroker must obtain a licence, or forfeit £25. The claimant did brokerage work for the defendant without a licence. In the absence of an express prohibition, the brokerage contract was held impliedly illegal since the object of the licences was to protect the public. Alternatively, the court may construe the contract and consider that the prohibition was introduced for an administrative purpose and not to forbid the contract in question; in *Learoyd v Bracken*, 1894, a statute required a stockbroker dealing in shares to issue a stamped contract note, or forfeit £20. It was held that a broker who failed to comply was entitled to recover his commission; "the object of the Act was not to vitiate the contract ... but to impose a penalty ... for the protection of the revenue," per Lopes LJ In modern statutes, the line is difficult to draw, as illustrated by *Archbolds (Freightage) Ltd v S. Spanglett Ltd*, CA, 1961.

It is necessary, before considering the effects of illegality (below), to distinguish between a contract that is,

(i)   illegal as formed; and

(ii) one that is illegal as performed.

In the case of (i), the very creation of the contract is forbidden, as in *Re Mahmoud* and *Cope v Rowlands* (above). In the case of (ii), the contract is lawful in its formation but performed by the parties in a manner that is illegal, as in *Ashmore, Benson, Pease Co Ltd v A.V. Dawson Ltd*, CA, 1973. Here, the claimants contracted with the defendant hauliers to carry a 25-ton load. The defendants used articulated lorries which by law were not permitted to carry more than 20 tonnes; the contract was held illegal in its performance. However, where the illegality is merely incidental to the performance of the contract, the contract may not be illegal at all; *St John Shipping Corp v Joseph Rank Ltd*, 1957. For example, in *Shaw v Groom*, CA, 1970, a rent book issued by a landlord failed to provide all the details required by statute. This did not prevent the landlord recovering arrears of rent from the tenant. The test would appear to be whether the illegality in the course of performance affects the "core" of the contract.

Contracts Illegal at Common Law on the Grounds of Public Policy

Certain contracts are regarded as illegal at common law on the grounds that, being injurious to society, they are contrary to public policy. Others, regarded as less damaging, are merely void (see below). It is questionable whether it is open to the courts to invent new heads of public policy. The contracts are as follows:

(1) Contracts to commit a crime, tort or fraud. Such a contract is illegal; examples include a contract between two highwaymen to ambush a coach (*Everet v Williams*, 1725), a contract to publish a libel (*Apthorp v Neville Co*, 1907) and a contract to purchase shares at inflated prices

and thereby rig the market (*Scott v Brown*, Doering, McNab Co, CA, 1892).

(2) Contracts promoting sexual immorality. A contract which directly or indirectly promotes such a purpose is illegal, such as in the next key case below.

(3) Contracts prejudicial to public safety. The principal examples of contracts illegal on this ground are: trading with an enemy alien in wartime, and contracts to perform acts which are illegal in a friendly foreign country; *Foster v Driscoll*, 1921.

(4) Contracts prejudicial to the administration of justice. As a general rule, a contract which involves stifling a prosecution is illegal and where an arrestable offence is concealed, a crime is thereby committed; Criminal Law Act 1967, s.5(1). However, there is authority that "private" offences such as assault may be lawfully compromised (*McGregor v McGregor*, CA, 1888), but the principle may not apply if the offence is a matter of public concern; *Keir v Leeman*, 1846. Agreements tending to defeat the bankruptcy laws have been held illegal; *Elliot v Richardson*, 1870.

(5) Contracts tending to promote corruption in public life. A contract to procure a public office or title will be illegal; *Parkinson v College of Ambulance*, 1925.

(6) Contracts to defraud the revenue. A contract which has as its objective the defrauding of the national or local revenue is illegal; *Miller v Karlinski*, CA, 1945.

KEY CASE

PEARCE V BROOKS, 1866
The claimants contracted to supply the defendant with a new carriage. As the claimants knew, the defendant was a prostitute who intended to use the carriage for the purposes of her business. The claimants sought payment.

Held: The action failed—the contract was unenforceable as indirectly promoting sexual immorality.

Comment
Attitudes to sexual morality have changed in modern times and in *Armhouse Lee Ltd v Chappell*, CA, 1996, a defence raised by pornographers that their trade was so immoral and illegal that they were not bound to pay for their advertising was dismissed.

Before considering the effects of illegality (below), it should be noted that the distinction between contracts illegal as formed and illegal as performed, discussed above, also applies to contracts illegal on the grounds of public policy.

Effects of Illegality

The first matter to be considered here is the state of mind of the parties. If the contract is illegal as formed (e.g. a contract to commit a crime or a contract expressly forbidden by statute), neither party will be able to sue or acquire rights under the contract. This is so even where the contract on the face of it appears to be legal but there is a common intention to achieve an illegal purpose. Where the contract is legal as formed but one party (and not the other) intends to exploit the contract for an illegal purpose, the innocent party may be able to sue on the contract; *Oom v Bruce*, 1810.

Thus the effects of illegality differ according to whether the contract is illegal as formed or illegal as performed.

1 Contract illegal as formed.

The effects are as follows:

(a) The contract is void and therefore neither party can sue upon it, ex turpi causa non oritur actio (no right of action arises from a base cause). It may be possible to circumvent this rule by bringing an action in misrepresentation; *Shelley v Paddock*, CA, 1980.

(b) Money paid or property transferred under the contract is not recoverable; *Taylor v Chester*, 1869. There are certain exceptions to this rule. First, where the party seeking recovery does not have to base his or her action on the illegal contract. Thus, where the claimants transferred machine tools to the defendants under hire-purchase contracts which were illegal, the defendants were held liable (in conversion) for having sold some of the tools. The wrongful sale had terminated the hire-purchase contracts and the claimants' action was brought as owner; *Bowmakers Ltd v Barnet Instruments Ltd*, CA, 1945. It seems that this exception also applies to a claim arising out of the contract under the law of trusts; *Tinsley v Milligan*, HL, 1993.

Secondly, where the parties have both participated in the illegal transaction but are not in pari delicto (not equally in the wrong), the less guilty party may be allowed to recover. This may be the case where the object of the statute is to protect a class of persons and the claimant is within the class: e.g. a tenant who pays an illegal premium may recover it; *Kiriri Cotton Co Ltd v Dewani*, PC, 1960. Thirdly, where the claimant repents before the illegal purpose has been fully performed, they may be allowed to recover; *Taylor v Bowers*, CA, 1876. In *Tribe v Tribe*, CA, 1996, the court indicated that "repentance" as such may not be necessary and it may be sufficient that the party merely withdraws from the illegal transaction.

(c) Related transactions will also be void. In *Fisher v Bridges*, 1854 a purchaser, who had bought land for an illegal purpose, executed a deed in respect of the balance of the purchase price. It was held no action lay on the deed as it was collateral to an illegal contract of sale. Where a third party enters into such a collateral contract his or her rights may depend upon the state of his or her knowledge as to the illegality; *Spector v Ageda*, 1971.

2 Illegal as performed.

Where the contract is lawful as formed, but where one party intends to exploit the contract to achieve an illegal purpose (i.e. one party is innocent and the other guilty), the position is as follows:

(a) The guilty party cannot sue on the contract for damages; *Cowan v Milbourn*, 1867;

(b) Money or property transferred by the guilty party cannot be recovered back by him or her unless the guilty party does not need to base his or her action on the illegal contract;

(c) The guilty party may be able to sue on a collateral contract that the main contract would be legally performed. In *Strongman Ltd v Sincock*, CA, 1955, the claimant builders carried out works under a contract with an architect. The architect had promised to obtain the necessary licences but failed to do so. The claimants were unable to sue on the main contract because of the illegality, nevertheless the architect was held liable under a collateral contract based on his promise. The innocent party, on the other hand, has full contractual remedies available to him or her, including the right to recover back money or property transferred.

In *Parkingeye Ltd v Somerfield Stores* one party's illegal method of performance was only an incidental part of the contract and did not have the effect of tainting the contract as a whole with illegality. In such a case, on the grounds of proportionality it would be unjust to leave the innocent party with no remedy in damages, particularly where the other party has wrongfully repudiated.

CONTRACTS VOID BY STATUTE

> ### LEGISLATION HIGHLIGHTER
>
> Certain contracts are expressly declared to be void by statute. Until recently, the most notable example was the wagering contract which was rendered void by the **Gaming Act 1845**. However this Act has been repealed by the **Gambling Act 2005** and the position now is that the fact that a contract related to gambling shall not prevent its enforcement. Certain types of restrictive trading agreements (regulated by the **Competition Act 1998**) are declared void; individual resale price maintenance agreements are considered in Chapter 12.

CONTRACTS VOID AT COMMON LAW

Certain contracts are considered to be void at common law on the grounds of public policy:

(1) Contracts to oust the jurisdiction of the courts. A contract is void in so far as it purports to deprive the courts of a jurisdiction which they otherwise would have, e.g. an agreement by a wife not to apply to the divorce court for maintenance is contrary to public policy; *Bennett v Bennett*, CA, 1952. The wife in such circumstances is not prevented from applying for maintenance; *Hyman v Hyman*, HL, 1929.

(2) Contracts prejudicial to the status of marriage. A contract is void where it restricts the person's freedom to marry (unless the restriction is mutual); *Lowe v Peers*, 1786. However, the validity of agreements between engaged couples or spouses for a possible future separation ("nuptial agreements") was recognised by the Supreme Court in *Radmacher v Granatino*, SC, 2010. A marriage brokerage contract (an agreement to procure the marriage of another) is void; *Hermann v Charlesworth*, CA, 1905.

(3) Contracts in restraint of trade. Contracts which are subject to the restraint of trade doctrine are prima facie void. The subject has generated more litigation than the other heads of public policy and will be dealt with more fully below.

CONTRACTS IN RESTRAINT OF TRADE

Certain contracts which impose a restriction on a person's right to carry on a trade or profession fall within the restraint of trade doctrine. All contracts falling within the doctrine are contrary to public policy and prima facie void, unless they can be regarded as reasonable as between the parties and as regards the public interest.

The burden of proving that, as between the parties, the restraint is reasonable, lies on the promisee; the burden of proving that, as far as the public interest is concerned, the restraint is unreasonable, lies on the promisor. Reasonableness is considered as at the time of the agreement.

The following transactions fall within the doctrine.

1 Agreements between employer and employee relating to the subsequent occupation of the employee
An agreement imposing a restriction on the employee after leaving an employer will only be reasonable between the parties if there is some proprietary interest of the employer meriting protection, i.e. trade secrets or business connection. The restriction must be no wider than reasonably necessary to protect such interest.

In *Forster v Suggett*, 1918, the defendant was employed as works manager of the claimant's glass works. He agreed that for five years after termination of employment with the claimants, he would not divulge any secret manufacturing process learnt during employment, nor would he work in the glass industry in the United Kingdom. It was held that the restraint was reasonable to protect the claimant's legitimate interest and was enforceable.

An employer may similarly protect his or her business connection if the employee is in a position of influence subsequently to entice away established customers, providing the restraint is no wider than reasonably necessary; *Herbert Morris Ltd v Saxelby*, HL, 1916. Restraints have been upheld against a milk roundsman, brewery manager and solicitor's clerk, but disallowed against a bookmaker's manager who had no personal contact with customers.

Occasionally, the courts are prepared to recognise other interests as meriting protection, apart from trade secrets and business connection. For example, in *Greig v Insole*, 1978, a professional cricketer sought to challenge a ban on cricketers who had joined a commercial "World Series". Slade J recognised that the governing bodies of cricket had a legitimate interest in ensuring that the game was properly administered; however, in the circumstances the ban was unreasonable. In this case, however, it should be noted that there was no contract between the cricketer and the governing bodies.

The restriction must also be reasonable as regards both area and duration. In *Mason v Provident Clothing Co Ltd*, HL, 1913, a restriction on a canvasser was held void as the area of restraint (25 miles of London) was one thousand times larger than the area of employment, and in *Fitch v Dewes*, 1921, a life-long restraint on a solicitor's managing clerk not to work within seven miles of Tamworth was held to be reasonable in the circumstances.

Exceptionally, agreements between an employer and employee will be held unreasonable as regards the public interest, i.e. where the community will be deprived of a valuable skill; *Wyatt v Kreglinger and Fernau*, CA, 1933. The courts are also prepared to invalidate indirect means of restraining employees; thus in *Kores Manufacturing Co Ltd v Kolok Manufacturing Co Ltd*, CA, 1959, two companies manufacturing similar products agreed that neither firm would employ a person who had been employed by the other in the previous five years. The agreement was held to be unreasonably wide as it failed to distinguish between employees privy to trade secrets and those who were not.

2 Agreements between the buyer and seller of a business
Restraints imposed upon the seller of a business to restrict competition are more readily upheld than restraints upon employees (above) but are generally subject to the same principles.

There must be a proprietary interest in need of protection; only the actual business sold is entitled to protection. In *British Reinforced Concrete Co v Schleff*, 1921, the claimant firm made and sold "BRC" road reinforcements. The defendants sold, but did not make, "Loop" road reinforcements. The claimants bought the defendants' business, with the defendants covenanting not to compete in the manufacture and sale of road reinforcements in the United Kingdom for a specified period. It was held that the restraint was unreasonably wide as it extended to manufacture instead of being confined to sale. The case also illustrates that a restraint on competition per se is void. For the same reason, a restriction which purports to restrain a business not actually carried on will be void: *Malt and Sake Brewing Co Ltd v Vancouver Breweries Ltd*, PC, 1934.

3 Agreements between manufacturers to restrict output and fix prices
Such agreements are prima facie void at common law but the courts have been prepared to uphold where reasonable, e.g. to avoid a glut on the market; *English Hop Growers v Dering*, CA, 1928. In fact such agreements are now almost entirely subject to statutory control under the Competition Act 1998; the Enterprise Act 2002; and arts 81 and 82 of the Treaty of Rome.

4 Exclusive dealing agreements
"Solus" agreements, whereby a garage agrees to purchase all its supply of petrol from one oil company, are within the doctrine of restraint of trade and are prima facie void.

Esso Petroleum Co Ltd v Harper's Garage (Stourport) Ltd, HL, 1968

The owner of two garages agreed, inter alia, to sell only Esso's petrol, in return for a rebate on the price per gallon. On one of the garages, the tie was to last for nearly four and a half years and on the other it was to last for 21 years, being contained in this case in a mortgage of the premises to Esso. The validity of the restraints was challenged.

Held: The four-and-a-half-year agreement was upheld as reasonable—although the agreement for 21 years was held to be unreasonable and void as being longer than necessary to protect Esso's legitimate interests, i.e. the continuity and stability of their marketing operation.

Comment

The court confirmed that, if a trader, when purchasing or leasing new premises, covenants with the vendor or lessor to buy only the latter's products, and then goes into possession, the exclusive dealing tie is outside the restraint of trade doctrine. This would apply, for example, to a person who buys or takes a lease of a public house or garage subject to a tie; the reason is that the person has surrendered no freedom previously enjoyed.

It should be noted that the common law relating to solus agreements is overlaid by statutory regulation under European and domestic law; unlike the common law, the scope of the relevant regulation is based on a test of market share.

Exclusive service agreements, such as where, for example, a songwriter agrees to provide his services for a music publisher for a period of time, are within the restraint of trade doctrine, (i.e. prima facie void) if oppressive and one-sided; *Schroeder Music Publishing Co Ltd v Macaulay*, HL, 1974.

Effects of the Contract Being Void

The effects discussed below relate to contracts void at common law an_
apply by analogy to contracts void by statute unless the statute in q_
has special provisions dealing with the matter.

The effects are as follows:

(1) The contract is void in so far as it contravenes public policy_
Day, 1837, a contract of employment contained a provisio_
alleged to be a void restraint of trade. This did not preven_
being able to recover arrears of salary. It follows

subsequent or collateral transactions are not necessarily void unless they relate solely to that part of the original transaction that is itself void.

(2) Money paid or property transferred is recoverable. Authority for this proposition is to be found in *Hermann v Charlesworth*, CA, 1905.

(3) Severance. Severance is the power of the court to remove a void provision in a contract and enforce the remainder. The power exists in the case of void contracts and there is authority that an illegal contract may be subjected to severance; *Carney v Herbert*, PC, 1985.

Severance will not be possible if it would eliminate the whole or substantially the whole of the consideration given by a party to the contract; *Wyatt v Kreglinger and Fernau*, CA, 1933. It may be possible to sever in the sense of removing the void part of a promise and enforcing the rest. This will be possible providing the severance does not alter the meaning of the contract in any way. In *Goldsoll v Goldman*, CA, 1915, the defendant sold a jewellery business to the claimant, the defendant covenanting that he would not deal in real or imitation jewellery in the United Kingdom or in other specified foreign places. The restraint as to the latter was too wide in the circumstances, as was the reference to real jewellery since the business dealt only in imitation jewellery in the United Kingdom. The void restrictions were severed leaving a valid contract in restraint of trade.

However, in *Attwood v Lamont*, CA, 1920, the defendant was employed as a tailoring cutter for the claimant, a general outfitter. The defendant covenanted not to subsequently engage in a number of trades carried on by the claimant's business, including tailor, milliner, draper, hatter and haberdasher, within a 10-mile radius. The court refused to sever so as to leave the ̄ng restriction valid; the covenant formed a single indivisible covenant ̄otection of the claimant's entire business. It was not a series of ̄ the protection of each department of the claimant's business. ̄ant was therefore void.

̄er be noted that, where severance applies, the court will ̄ in any way, thus applying the so-called "blue pencil ̄ strike out the offending words; what is left must ̄ditions.

̄: Restraint of Trade

̄e in restraint of trade cases is the ̄ch to construction.

ILLEGAL AND VOID CONTRACTS

145

d will estion

In *Wallis v* which was the claimant that from this

LITTLEWOODS ORGANISATION LTD V HARRIS, CA, 1978

Harris was a director of the mail-order firm, Littlewoods. He entered into a restraint clause whereby he agreed not to work for the GUS group of companies for 12 months after leaving Littlewoods. Harris had acquired confidential information in relation to Littlewoods mail-order catalogue. GUS were Littlewoods' main rival in the domestic mail-order business; however, GUS operated worldwide and their business was not confined to mail order, whereas Littlewoods only operated in the United Kingdom. The validity of the clause was challenged.

Held: Although the clause, on its literal wording, was too wide, by construing the clause with reference to circumstances existing when the contract was made, it was possible to limit it to those matters it was clearly intended to protect, i.e. the mail order business in the United Kingdom. The clause was therefore a valid restraint of trade.

Comment

As a consequence of the *Littlewoods* decision, the court may reach a different conclusion dependent upon whether it adopts the literal or flexible approach to construction. This dilemma is illustrated by apparently conflicting subsequent decisions, e.g. *J A Mont (UK) Ltd v Mills*, CA, 1993 and *Hanover Insurance Brokers Ltd v Schapiro*, CA, 1994.

Figure 20: Contracts in Restraint of Trade

REVISION CHECKLIST

You should now know and understand:

☐ those circumstances in which a contract may be illegal by statute;

☐ the situations in which the contract will be illegal at common law on the grounds of public policy;

☐ the circumstances in which a contract will be void by statute and at common law;

☐ contracts in restraint of trade.

QUESTION AND ANSWER

Peter and Laura were two highly trained store detectives who worked for Securit plc, a retail security firm operating in London and the Home Counties. Peter was the chief store detective whose job mainly entailed the negotiation of new contracts with customers of Securit plc.

The detectives' contracts of employment contained the following clause: "For one year after termination of employment with Securit plc, a store detective shall not work for any other business organistion in the United Kingdom as a detective nor compete, in any way, with Securit plc in retail security."

Peter and Laura then decided to leave Securit plc and terminated their employment with the firm having given due notice.

Six months after leaving Securit plc, Laura took a job as a store detective in London. At the same time, Peter started a business providing a range of security services for businesses in London.

Advise Securit plc.

ADVICE AND THE ANSWER

General guidance

Illegality is generally regarded as one of the more difficult topics in contract law. It can involve fine distinctions, for example, the difference between a contract illegal *as formed* and a contract illegal *as performed* is particularly thorny.

The above question deals with contracts in restraint of trade, a topic that has spawned a considerable amount of case law and frequently appears on examination papers as either a problem or essay question. Problem questions on the topic are likely to involve the issue of severance, i.e. to what extent can a void restraint be severed from the contract so that it may be enforced. As discussed earlier in this chapter, the traditional approach to such clauses involves the application of a strict blue pencil test.

The more flexible approach in *Littlewoods v Harris* achieves the same objective by rendering enforceable a clause that would otherwise be struck down because of its width, providing it is reasonable between the parties and as regards the public interest. Good answers should consider both approaches, where relevant, but the difficulty at the moment is that the law is in a state of uncertainty as to whether, and it what circumstances, the flexible approach is permissible.

Answer plan

1 The answer should begin with the observation that contracts falling within the restraint of trade doctrine are prima facie void unless reasonable as between the parties and in the interests of the public; Lord Macnaghten in *Nordenfelt v Maxim Nordenfelt Guns and Ammunition Co Ltd*, HL, 1894. If the restraint clause is valid, Securit plc may be able to prevent either Peter or Laura from breaching it by obtaining an injunction.

2 An agreement imposing a restriction on an employee after leaving an employer will only be reasonable as between the parties if the employer has some proprietary interest meriting protection. The restriction must be no wider than reasonably necessary to protect such interest. The interests qualifying for protection are (i) trade secrets and (ii) business connection.

3 Neither Peter nor Laura appear to be privy to trade secrets and so the question therefore is whether either has acquired business connection so that they may be in a position where they may be able to entice away established customers of Securit plc.

4 It is not every employee who can be validly restrained in this way— they must not only be in contact with customers but they must be in a position to have some influence over them, e.g. *Fitch v Dewes*, 1921 (solicitor's clerk) and *Home Counties Dairies Ltd v Skilton*, 1970 (milk roundsman).

5 It is arguable on the facts that against Laura there is no proprietary interest to protect, given her status in the firm. If that were the case, the clause would be unreasonable and unenforceable against Laura. With regard to Peter, there does appear to be a proprietary interest, given the influence he may have over customers.

6 The next question is the wording of the clause. Restraint clauses must be reasonable as regards duration and geographical area. They must also not be too wide in terms of the business or activity restrained. With regard to duration, it depends on the circumstances— as against Peter, 12 months may not be unreasonably long.

7 However, the clause is clearly too wide in terms of geographical area (eg *Mason v Provident Clothing*) as it refers to the UK. The reference to working for any other business as a detective and the restraint on competing in any way in retail security extend beyond the scope of the employer's business; *Commercial Plastics Ltd v Vincent*, CA, 1964.

8 Given the width of the clause, severance will not be possible as what is left after striking out the offending words will have no meaning. Can the flexible approach be applied? In *Littlewoods v Harris*, the Court of Appeal was prepared to uphold a clause which was wider than reasonably necessary to protect the relevant interest.

9 However, in *Littlewoods*, it was possible to discern the parties' intentions from the factual background to the case; and in any event the restraint only extended to a specified competitor.

10 Whereas this approach is theoretically feasible in this case, the fact that the clause involves a general restraint, and in view of the doubts expressed in *Mont v Mills*, the better view is that the literal approach should be adhered to. In *Mont v Mills*, the court did not consider that it should investigate whether there was some implicit limitation in the clause which rendered it less wide that its literal wording.

Privity of Contract

INTRODUCTION

In this chapter we consider the common law rule of privity which treats a contract as essentially a private affair in which third parties acquire neither rights nor liabilities even though they may have some interest which may be served by the performance of the contract. The rule is subject to various exceptions both statutory and at common law. The main elements are:

1   A major statutory exception in the Contracts (Rights of Third Parties) Act 1999 where a third party may enforce a contract made for their benefit

2   The position where the action is brought by the promisee

3   The established exceptions to the doctrine

> ### CHECKPOINT
>
> The rule of privity means that, in general, a person who is not privy to a contract, that is, a third party, can neither sue nor be sued on that contract.

Where the rule prevents the burden of a contract being imposed on a third party, it is both sensible and just. Thus, in *Dunlop Pneumatic Tyre Co v Selfridge Co Ltd*, HL, 1915, the claimants sold tyres to Dew and Co, wholesale distributors, on terms that Dew and Co would obtain an undertaking from retailers that they would not sell below the claimant's list price. Dew and Co sold some of the tyres to the defendants, who retailed them below list price and the claimants sought an injunction and damages. The action failed because although there was a contract between Dew and Co and the defendants, the claimants were not a party to it and so the obligation they sought to impose on the defendants was unenforceable.

The rule of privity is less easy to justify where a contract between A and B is intended to confer a benefit on a third party, C. In such a situation C cannot enforce the contract because

(i)   they are not privy to the contract between A and B; and

(ii)   C has not provided consideration (see *Tweddle v Atkinson*, Chapter 4).

Legislative reform to allow the third party to sue was first mooted over 70 years ago and there have been a number of judicial assaults upon the doctrine.

Figure 21: Dunlop v Selfridge

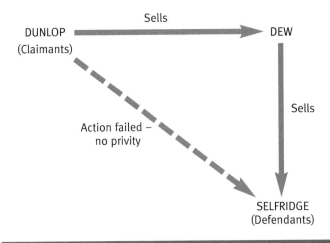

KEY CASE

BESWICK V BESWICK, HL, 1968
A coal merchant agreed to sell his business to his nephew, who in return agreed to pay a weekly sum to his uncle, and after the uncle's death a weekly sum would be payable to the uncle's widow. Ultimately, the widow brought an action against the nephew for arrears of the weekly sum and for specific performance of the agreement. She sued (i) as administratrix of her deceased husband's estate; and (ii) in her personal capacity, relying on s.56(1) of the **Law of Property Act 1925**. The Court of Appeal sought to rely on s.56(1) in order to avoid the privity rule. The subsection provides that a person may acquire an interest in land or other property, or the benefit of a covenant relating to land or other property, although not actually named as a party in the conveyance or other document. Further, s.205(1) provides that, unless the context otherwise requires, the word "property" means any interest in real or personal property. Liberally interpreted, these provisions could present a means of evading the doctrine of privity, particularly if the reference to "other property" could embrace contractual rights. The Court of Appeal held that she was entitled as administratrix to an order of specific performance; a majority of the court found that she could also succeed in her personal capacity by virtue of s.56(1). The nephew appealed.

Held: The widow's claim as administratrix was good and she was entitled to specific performance since damages would be an inadequate remedy. Her personal claim should fail as s.56(1) was limited to transactions involving realty; there was a presumption that the **Law of Property Act 1925**, being a consolidating Act, did not fundamentally alter the common law by a "sidewind".

Comment
Despite the outcome of this case, judicial criticism of the rule continued, and in 1996 the Law Commission put forward draft legislation; this, after some amendment, became the **Contracts (Rights of Third Parties) Act 1999**. The provisions of the Act are dealt with below.

The rule of privity is subject to a number of exceptions at common law, in equity and by statute. The statutory exceptions and the 1999 Act will be considered first.

Statutory Exceptions

There are a number of statutory exceptions which include the following: under the Law of Property Act 1925, s.136, it is possible to assign rights arising under a contract; under the Bills of Exchange Act 1882, s.29, a third party may sue on a bill of exchange or cheque and under the Married Woman's Property Act 1882, s.11, as amended, a spouse may obtain the benefit of a contract of life assurance which is made for the benefit of the other spouse. None of the established statutory exceptions are affected by the 1999 Act; however, the enforceable third party right created by the Act is itself a major exception to privity.

CONTRACTS (RIGHTS OF THIRD PARTIES) ACT 1999

LEGISLATION HIGHLIGHTER

The fundamental change to the common law brought about by the 1999 Act is to be found in s.1(1) and 1(2). Section 1(1) of the Act states:

"Subject to the provisions of this Act, a person who is not a party to the contract (a 'third party') may in his own right enforce a term of the contract if—
(a) the contract expressly provides that he may, or
(b) subject to subsection (2), the term purports to confer a benefit on him."

However, subs.(2) provides that s.1(1)(b) above will "not apply if on a proper construction of the contract it appears that the parties did not intend the term to be enforceable by the third party".

In the first reported case under the Act, *Nisshin Shipping Co Ltd v Cleaves*, 2003, it was held that the effect of s.1(2) was to provide that s.1(1)(b) was disapplied if on a proper construction it appeared that the parties did not intend third party enforcement. If the contract was neutral on the question, s.1(2) did not disapply s.1(1)(b). This interpretation was confirmed by the Court of Appeal in *Laemthong International Lines Co Ltd v Artis*, CA, 2005. In *Prudential Assurance Co v Ayres*, 2007 it was held that there was nothing in s.1(1)(b) which required the benefit to the third party to be the predominant purpose or intent behind the term. On the other hand, s.1(1)(b) was not disapplied if the benefit is conferred on someone other than the third party.

The third party must be expressly identified in the contract by name, as a member of a class or as answering a particular description but need not be in existence when the contract is entered into (s.1(3)).

Once it is established that the third party has an enforceable right, the Act makes available to him or her any remedy available to a party to the contract, e.g. damages, injuction or specific performance (s.1(5)). Likewise, they may take the benefit of an exclusion or limitation clause (s.1(6)).

Variation and Rescission

The parties to the contract may not, unless the agreement otherwise provides, rescind or vary the beneficial term to the detriment of the third party if:

(1) the third party has communicated, by words or conduct, his assent to the relevant term to the promisor;

(2) the promisor is aware that the third party has relied on the relevant term; or

(3) the promisor can reasonably be expected to have foreseen that the third party would rely on the relevant term and the third party has in fact relied on it (s.2(1), (2) and (3)).

Defences

Section 3 provides that the promisor may, unless the contract otherwise provides, raise against the third party any defence or set-off that could have been raised against the promisee. The above provision means that the third party will be no more able to enforce a void, discharged or unenforceable contract than the promisee could.

The Act also provides (s.3(4)) that the promisor may rely on defences, set-offs or counterclaims against the third party which do not arise from the contract itself but from previous dealings. A third party can only rely on any exclusion or limitation clause if he could have done so had he been a party to the contract (s.3(6)).

Finally, s.5 provides that where the promisee has recovered damages from the promisor in respect of the third party's loss, the court shall reduce any award to the third party to take account of the sum already recovered.

Exceptions

Section 6 prescribes a number of contracts which are specifically excepted from the provisions of the Act. These include bills of exchange and promissory notes, terms in contracts of employment against an employee, terms in contracts for the carriage of goods by sea other than clauses of exclusion or limitation (and certain other contracts of carriage other than clauses of exclusion and limitation). This means that a third party may rely on an exclusion clause without having to rely on the agency device in *New Zealand Shipping Co Ltd v A.M. Satterthwaite Co Ltd*, PC, 1975 (see Chapter 7).

Effect of the Legislation

Section 7(1) provides that the Act "does not affect any right or remedy of a third party that exists or is available apart from this Act"; thus the Act does not replace any of the established judicial exceptions to privity. It may mean, however, that the third parties in cases such as *Beswick v Beswick* will be able to bring an action in their own right. Nevertheless, as we have seen, it will be perfectly possible for the parties to the contract to exclude the operation of the statute.

Before considering the established exceptions to privity, it is necessary to examine the position at common law where the promisee brings an action to enforce a term of the contract which benefits a third party. This possibility pre-dates the 1999 Act and is unaffected by the new legislation.

. . . .

ACTION BROUGHT BY PROMISEE

Where A contracts with B to confer a benefit on C, we have seen that C has no rights at common law because of the privity rule. Unless there is agency or a trust (see below), at common law the only means by which the contract may be enforced will be if one of the contracting parties themselves sues. The problem here is that in many cases damages will be the usual remedy, unless specific performance is ordered, as in *Beswick v Beswick*. In strict theory the damages will only be nominal since the claimant, as a contracting party, will have suffered no loss.

In *Jackson v Horizon Holidays Ltd*, CA, 1975, the claimant contracted with the defendants for a holiday for himself and his family which turned out to be disastrous. The claimant recovered substantial damages to cover not only his own disappointment, but also that of his wife and children. Lord Denning MR was of the view, relying on a dictum in *Lloyds v Harper*, CA, 1880, that the contracting party in such circumstances can recover substantial damages to cover the third party's loss. This view was corrected by the House of Lords in *Woodar Investment Development Ltd v Wimpey Construction UK Ltd*, HL, 1980 as being too wide. The decision in *Jackson* was justified by the House on the basis the claimant's damages reflected his own disappointment at the ruined family holiday or as a special category of case where contracts are arranged by one person for a group.

Another exception to the general rule was allowed in *Linden Gardens Trust Ltd v Lanesta Sludge Disposals Ltd*, HL, 1994. X employed Y to carry out work on his land, in circumstances where it was understood that X was likely to transfer the property to Z. The work of Y was defective and in breach of contract. Although X no longer had any interest in the property, the House of Lords awarded substantial damages; per Lord Browne-Wilkinson, it seems proper "to treat the parties as having entered the contract on the footing that [the original owner] would be entitled to enforce the contractual rights for the benefit of those who suffered from defective performance". Nevertheless, in *Alfred McAlpine Construction Ltd v Panatown Ltd*, HL, 2000, the House of Lords debarred the employer in a building contract, by reason of the fact that it was not the owner of the land, from recovering substantial damages where the owner had a direct right to sue the contractor. Thus, there was no necessity to depart from the general rule that substantial damages cannot be recovered by a promisee suffering no loss.

Figure 22: Enforcement by Promisee

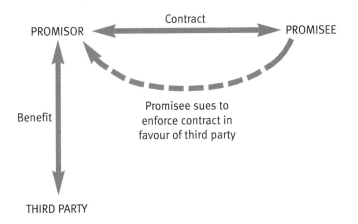

ESTABLISHED EXCEPTIONS

Agency

Agency is a major common law exception to the doctrine of privity. A contract of agency arises where one person (the principal) appoints an agent to enter into contracts on his or her behalf with third parties. As a general rule, the principal, even if undisclosed, may sue the third party. An example of agency being used to circumvent the privity rule is to be seen in *New Zealand Shipping Co Ltd v A. M. Satterthwaite Co Ltd*, PC, 1975 (see Chapter 7). Once the agent has brought about a contract between the principal and third party, the agent drops out of the transaction.

Figure 23: Agency

Collateral Contract

The collateral contract device, whilst not strictly an exception, may be used to evade the privity rule.

KEY CASE

SHANKLIN PIER LTD v DETEL PRODUCTS LTD, 1951

The claimants employed contractors to repaint their pier and specified that the defendants' (i.e. Detel's) paint was to be used. The defendants had previously represented to the claimants that the paint would last from 7 to 10 years. The defendants sold the paint to the contractors and it was used but it only lasted three months. The claimants sought damages from the defendants.

Held: Although the claimants could not sue on the contract for the sale of the paint, to which they were not a party, it was found that they could successfully sue the defendants on a collateral contract arising from their promise as to the longevity of the paint.

Comment
The claimants' consideration to enforce this promise consisted of their causing the contractors to enter into a contract to buy paint from the defendants.

Covenants Which Run with the Land

The position in land law is that burdens imposed on land may in certain circumstances "run with the land" and be enforceable against subsequent owners; *Smith and Snipes Hall Farm v River Douglas Catchment Board*, CA, 1949. Similarly, covenants in leases may, providing certain conditions are satisfied, likewise run with the land. In equity, under the doctrine of *Tulk v Moxhay*, 1848, a restrictive covenant may run with the land; thus if A buys land from B, promising not to build thereon, and A later sells to C, C may be bound by the restriction. For the restriction to be enforceable against C, two major conditions must be satisfied:

(i)   C must have had notice of the restriction at the time of purchase; and

(ii) B must have retained land capable of benefiting from the restriction.

Restrictions on Price

At common law, suppliers were prevented from restricting the price at which goods were resold by the doctrine of privity (see *Dunlop v Selfridge*, above).

The position is now regulated by statute. By virtue of the Competition Act 1998, any attempt by a supplier to fix a minimum price at which goods are resold is void.

Restrictions upon the Use of Chattels

The question has arisen whether the principle in *Tulk v Moxhay* (above) may be applied to personalty, so as to render a restriction upon the use of a chattel enforceable against a subsequent owner who is not party to the original contract.

In *Lord Strathcona Steamship Co v Dominion Coal Co*, PC, 1926, the respondents chartered the ship SS Strathcona for use on the St Lawrence River for several summer seasons. During the period of the charter party, the ship was sold to the appellants who took with notice of the charter. They subsequently refused to permit the respondents to use the ship in accordance with the charter party. An injunction was granted to restrain the appellants from using the ship in a manner inconsistent with the charter party. The Privy Council in this case placed much reliance on the principle in *Tulk v Moxhay*. This, however, is open to the objection that the charterers lacked the proprietary interest necessary to enforce a restrictive covenant under *Tulk v Moxhay*. Further, in *Clore v Theatrical Properties Ltd*, CA, 1936, the Court of Appeal said that the *Strathcona* decision should be confined to the particular case of the charter party of a ship, and in *Port Line Ltd v Ben Line Steamers Ltd*, 1958, Diplock J considered that *Strathcona* was wrongly decided.

In fact, the case has met with some more recent approval, although not on the restrictive covenant theory. In *Swiss Bank Corp v Lloyds Bank Ltd*, 1979, Browne-Wilkinson J took the view that the appellants in *Strathcona* were in the position of constructive trustees, or alternatively, the principle in the case was the "counterpart in equity" of the tort of knowingly interfering with contractual relations. Although this may be indicative of the way the law will develop, as things stand at present, *Strathcona*, even if correctly decided, is of limited application.

The Trust Device

One means of evading the doctrine of privity is to show that, where A contracts with B to confer a benefit on C, one of the contracting parties, say B, is holding their contractual rights on trust for C. In such a case, C may be able to ask B to sue as trustee; in the event of a refusal, C may bring proceedings joining the trustee as co-defendant. The trust device in this context can be traced to *Gregory and Parker v Williams*, 1817 and had become firmly established by the time of *Les Affreteurs Reunis SA v Walford*, HL, 1919. In this case, Walford, a broker, arranged a charter party between ship owners and charterers. The charter party contained a term by which the ship owners promised to pay Walford three per cent commission on the value of the hire. Although Walford was not privy to the contract between the charterers and the ship owners, the House of Lords held that the charterers were to be regarded as trustees for Walford and they could therefore enforce payment of the commission against the ship owners.

No formal words are required to create such a trust but there must be the intention to create a trust, although "an intention to provide benefits for someone else and pay them does not of itself give rise to a trusteeship", per Romer LJ in *Green v Russell*, CA, 1959. The device depends largely on the readiness of the court to construe a trust and many of the decided cases are inconsistent. The judicial tide seems to have turned against the trust device in *Re Schebsman*, CA, 1943, where Schebsman's employers agreed to pay him an annual sum, or, if he died, payment would be made to his wife and daughter. The Court of Appeal, in holding that there was no trust, was influenced by the fact that Schebsman and his employers were at liberty to vary consensually the terms of the agreement; this would not have been possible had the contract created a trust.

It is noteworthy that in *Beswick v Beswick*, HL, 1968, (see above) where the facts were not dissimilar to *Re Schebsman*, the Court of Appeal were of the view that no trust could be inferred in favour of the third party and the matter was not canvassed before the House of Lords.

You should now know and understand:

- [ ] the operation of the Contracts (Rights of Third Parties) Act 1999;
- [ ] the position, in relation to privity, where the action is brought by the promisee;
- [ ] the established exceptions to privity.

QUESTION AND ANSWER

THE QUESTION

"[N]o stranger to the consideration can take advantage of a contract, although made for his benefit." (Wightman J in *Tweddle v Atkinson*, 1861)

Consider how far the above statement continues to have validity in the light of the passing of the Contracts (Rights of Third Parties) Act 1999, examining the machinery of the Act itself.

ADVICE AND THE ANSWER

General guidance

Questions on privity of contract nowadays are likely to involve some consideration of the Act of 1999. The Act creates a statutory exception to the long-established rule that a stranger to a contract cannot enforce it even where made for his benefit. However, it is important to note that the Act does not do away with the fundamental rule of privity regarding the enforcement of the benefit of a contract by a third party, but it does introduce a substantial exception to it. The basic rule should be retained as there will be cases where the parties to the contract simply do not intend the third party to enforce the contract. So far as the privity rule prevents the *burden* of a contract being imposed on a third party, the 1999 Act does not impact on this principle. As the following plan illustrates, in order adequately to address the issues in the question, it is important to have a detailed grasp of the statutory provisions.

Answer plan

1 A useful starting point for the answer would be to consider the case of *Tweddle v Atkinson* itself, where A entered into a contract with B that A and B would confer a benefit on C. The stranger to the contract, C, was unable to enforce it. This was so even though the contract expressly provided provided that C should "have full power to sue [A and B] in any court of law and equity". (However, this wording, if used after the passing of the Act of 1999, may well be sufficient to render the third party right under the Act enforceable).

2 The principle was later confirmed by the House of Lords in *Dunlop Pneumatic Tyre Co Ltd v Selfridge & Co Ltd*. A more determined assault was made on the rule by the Court of Appeal in *Beswick v Beswick* but ultimately the House of Lords upheld it. The impetus for reform came from the Law Commission in their report of 1996.

3 Section 1 of the Act enables the enforcement of third party rights. It provides that a person who is not a party to the contract may in his own right enforce a term if (a) the contract expressly provides that he may; or (b) the term purports to confer a benefit on him, unless on a proper construction of the contract it appears that the parties did not intend the term to be enforceable by a third party.

4 Thus to make sure that the third party will be able to enforce the benefit (under (a) above) it should say so explicitly in the contract. A slightly less certain route is provided by (b) above, but may assist those without the benefit of legal advice. It seems that any rebuttal of the presumption of enforceability under (b) must be made in clear terms; *Nisshin Shipping Co Ltd v Cleaves*, 2003. If the contract is neutral on the matter the presumption will not be disapplied.

5 Under s.1(3), the third party must be expressly identified in the contract by name, as a member of a class or as answering to a particular description but need not be in existence when the contract was entered into.

6 The range of beneficiaries is therefore restricted but it does confer rights on children yet to be born, spouses yet to marry or incorporated bodies not yet formed. However, the rights must be conferred by contract and not, e.g. by will. A third party must be identified in the contract; *Avraamides v Colwill*, CA, 2006.

7 It should be noted that the common rule that "consideration must move from the promise" has not been abolished by the Act but it does not apply where a third party has an enforceable contractual right under the Act.

8 Once it is established that a third party has an enforceable right, the Act makes available to them any remedy that would have been available to them on an action for breach of contract, eg damages, injunction etc; and they may take the benefit of an exclusion clause.

9 At common law the parties to the contract are free to vary or rescind the terms of the contract as they wish. This could allow the contracting parties to make a later agreement to reduce or even cancel the third parties' benefit.

10 Accordingly, there is machinery in s.2 of the Act preventing rescission or variation of the original contract where the third party communicates to the promisor his assent to the relevant term or the third party has relied on the term and the promisor is aware of, or has foreseen, that fact. Nevertheless the underlying freedom of contract position is preserved in that the parties may include a term that the contract may be rescinded or varied without the third party's consent.

11 Section 3 of the Act provides that the promisor may, unless the contract otherwise provides, raise against the third party any defence or set-off that could have been raised by the promisee. Thus, as far as the enforceability of the beneficial term is concerned, under the Act, the third party is in the same position as the promisee would have been. Further, the promisor may rely on defences, set-offs or counter-claims which do not arise from the contract itself but from previous dealings.

12 Under s.5, where the promisee has recovered substantial damages in respect of the third party's loss, and the third party has an enforceable right under s.1, this will be taken into account in any proceedings brought by the third party. Thus any award to the third party will be reduced by the court to the extent considered appropriate.

13 There are some categories of contract that are exempted by s.6. These include negotiable instruments; certain contracts under the Companies Act 1985; limited liability partnership agreements; and terms in employment contracts. It should be noted that the Act does not create any enforceable third party rights in the case of certain contracts of carriage other than clauses of exclusion and limitation.

14 There is an important provision in s.7 of the Act which states that the Act "does not affect any right or remedy of a third party that exists or is available apart from this Act"—established judicial exceptions to the Act will continue to exist as will the various statutory exceptions to the rule.

15 A good summary might observe that the Act will improve the position of third parties, who, under the traditional rule of privity have been denied the right to enforce a contract made for their benefit. The Act is likely to prove most helpful to those contracting parties who *intend* to benefit a third party; providing they make their intention clear in the contract, the third party will have a remedy. Nevertheless, the ease with which provisions of the Act may be excluded will enable the draftsman to ensure that unintended beneficiaries may be excluded.

Discharge of Contract

. . . .

INTRODUCTION

In the early part of this book we examined the way that contracts come into existence. We are concerned in this chapter with the way in which contracts are brought to an end, ie the discharge of contracts. Discharge may occur:

1 Under the doctrine of frustration
2 By a serious breach of the contract
3 By the parties agreeing to discharge the contract
4 Through the contract being performed

These matters will be dealt with in turn.

. . . .

FRUSTRATION

> **CHECKPOINT**
>
> Under the doctrine of frustration, a contract may be automatically discharged if, during the currency of the contract, and without the fault of either party, some event occurs which renders further performance an impossibility, renders it illegal or brings about a radical change in the circumstances so that the contract becomes something essentially different from that which was originally undertaken.

Juristic Basis

It is necessary to establish the juristic basis of the doctrine in order to apply the correct legal test for discovering whether the contract has been frustrated. There are two main theories:

1 Implied term theory

This theory stems from *Taylor v Caldwell*, HL, 1863 and *F. A. Tamplin S. S. v Anglo Mexican Petroleum*, HL, 1916. In these cases it was said that the contract was to be regarded as being subject to an implied term that the parties shall be excused if performance were to become impossible by virtue of some event which is the fault of neither party. The theory has been criticised as artificial and the second of the two theories is now generally preferred.

2 Radical change in the obligation

This test was favoured by the majority of the House of Lords in *Davis Contractors Ltd v Fareham UDC*, HL, 1956. Per Lord Radcliffe: "there must be such a change in the significance of the obligation that the thing undertaken would, if performed, be a different thing from that contracted for". The test is objective; discharge occurs automatically upon the frustrating event and does not depend on any repudiation by the parties.

Frustrating Events

The situations in which a contract might become frustrated cannot be exhaustively listed but the cases may be categorised under the following heads.

1 Impossibility

A contract may become impossible to perform where the subject-matter is destroyed. In *Taylor v Caldwell*, the claimant agreed to hire a music hall from the defendant for the purpose of holding concerts on specified dates. Before the first of these dates and without the fault of either party, the hall was destroyed by fire. It was held that the contract was discharged by frustration.

Similarly a contract may be frustrated if the subject-matter becomes, through some extraneous cause, unavailable, as where a ship required for the performance of the contract is stranded; *Nickoll and Knight v Ashton Eldridge Co*, 1901. The unavailability of a person required for the performance of a contract may similarly frustrate it; *Morgan v Manser*, 1948. In any case of unavailability, whether the contract is frustrated may depend on the length of the period of time of the unavailability. Other factors include: the terms of the contract; the parties' assumptions at the time of the contract; and the nature of the supervening event (*Edwinton Commercial Corp v Tsavliris Russ Ltd*, CA, 2007).

Where a particular method of performance becomes impossible, the contract will only be frustrated where the method is essential to the performance of the contract and it was expressly or impliedly stipulated for in the contract itself. In *Tsakiroglou Co Ltd v Noblee Thorl GmbH*, HL, 1962, the closure of the Suez Canal did not frustrate a contract to ship groundnuts despite the fact that the parties anticipated they would be shipped via Suez. The House of Lords refused to imply a term to that effect since the voyage round the Cape was not commercially fundamentally different.

2 Illegality

If, during the currency of the contract, a change in the law renders further performance illegal, the contract will be frustrated. Thus, the outbreak of hostilities may render the further performance of a trading contract illegal as "trading with the enemy".

3 Radical change in the circumstances

Exceptionally, frustration may occur where, due to some extraneous event, further performance, though technically possible, would become something radically different from that originally envisaged by the parties.

KEY CASE

KRELL V HENRY, CA, 1903

The claimant agreed to let a room to the defendant for coronation day. It was understood by both parties that the purpose of the letting was to view the procession. The coronation was cancelled owing to the illness of the King.

Held: The contract was frustrated as the viewing of the procession was the "foundation of the contract".

Comment

In another "coronation case", a contract for the hire of a steamboat for viewing the King's naval review and for a cruise around the fleet was held not to be frustrated by the cancellation of the review. The review was not regarded as the foundation of the contract; *Herne Bay Steam Boat Co v Hutton*, CA, 1903.

A contract will not be frustrated where a change of circumstances renders it more onerous to perform but not radically different. In *Davis Contractors Ltd v Fareham UDC*, HL, 1956, the House of Lords refused to hold a building contract frustrated where, because of labour shortages, the work took three times longer than had been agreed. The same principle was applied to the impact of the 2008 global economic downturn in *Tandrin Aviation Holdings Ltd v Aero Toy Store LLC*, 2010.

The courts have traditionally been reluctant to apply the doctrine of frustration to leaseholds, as a lease creates an estate in the land. In *Cricklewood Property and Investment Trust Ltd v Leighton's Investment Trust Ltd*, HL, 1945, the House of Lords was evenly divided on the matter, but in *National Carriers Ltd v Panalpina (Northern) Ltd*, HL, 1981 the House decided, by a majority, that a lease could be frustrated, although only very rarely.

LIVERPOOL JOHN MOORES UNIVERSITY
LEARNING SERVICES

Limits to Frustration

The courts have imposed certain limits on the doctrine:

(1) Self-induced frustration. Where the alleged "frustrating" event is brought about by the fault of one of the parties, the "frustration" is said to be self-induced and the party at fault will be liable for breach of contract. The contract will not be discharged by frustration. An example is where one party elects to pursue a course of action that renders performance impossible; *Maritime National Fish Ltd v Ocean Trawlers Ltd*, PC, 1935; *Super Servant Two*, CA, 1990; and *Bunge SA v Kyla Shipping Co Ltd*, CA, 2013. The onus of proving the frustration is self-induced lies on the party so alleging.

(2) Express provision. A contract may contain an express provision dealing with the possibility of a frustrating event which then in fact occurs. If this is the case, the doctrine of frustration does not apply and the risks are allocated in accordance with the terms of the contract (illegality excepted). Such provisions are construed narrowly; *Metropolitan Water Board v Dick Kerr Co Ltd*, HL, 1918.

(3) Event foreseen. If one party foresaw or should have foreseen the "frustrating" event by reason of his or her own special knowledge, the doctrine of frustration does not apply and that party will be liable for breach of contract; *Walton Harvey Ltd v Walker and Homfrays Ltd*, CA, 1931. There is authority for the proposition that if both parties foresaw or should have foreseen the event, but made no provision in the contract to deal with it, the contract may nevertheless be frustrated; *W.J. Tatem Ltd v Gamboa*, 1939. However, the less that an event is foreseeable, the more likely it is to be a factor, depending on other factors, which may lead to frustration; *Edwinton Commercial Corpn v Tsavliris Russ*, CA, 2007.

Legal Effect of Frustration

The effect of frustration is to discharge the contract automatically as to the future, but not to render it void ab initio (cf. the effect of an operative mistake; see Chapter 9).

The result is that, at common law, the rights and liabilities of the parties existing before the frustrating event are preserved, thus "the loss lies where it falls". The harsh consequence of this at common law was that money paid by one party to the other before the frustrating event could not be recovered, and money payable before the frustration remained payable. Thus, in *Chandler v Webster*, CA, 1904, the claimant agreed to hire a room in Pall Mall from the defendant to watch the coronation procession. The contract price was £141 payable immediately. The claimant paid a deposit of £100 but before he paid the balance the contract was frustrated by the cancellation of the procession. The court held that not only could the claimant not recover the £100 but he was liable for the balance of £41 as the obligation to pay the whole contract price had fallen due before frustration.

Figure 24: Chandler v Webster

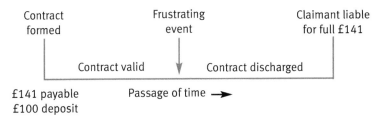

The rigid rule in *Chandler v Webster* was modified by the House of Lords in the following case.

KEY CASE

FIBROSA S.A. v FAIRBAIRN LAWSON COMBE BARBOUR LTD, HL, 1943
An English company agreed to sell machinery to a Polish company, with a deposit of one-third of the purchase price being payable at the time of the agreement. The sum of £1,000 was paid but, before any machinery was delivered, war broke out and the contract was frustrated.

Held: Overruling *Chandler v Webster*—that the Polish company was entitled to recover the deposit paid, on the ground of a total failure of consideration (a form of quasi-contract). Money had been paid to secure performance and there had been no performance.

Comment
The law was still unsatisfactory in that (i) there was no remedy where the failure of consideration was only partial; and (ii) it did not provide for the situation where the payee had incurred expenses in reliance on the contract (as the English company had done in *Fibrosa*). These injustices led to legislation.

Figure 25: Appleby v Myers

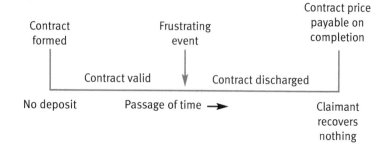

The Law Reform (Frustrated Contracts) Act 1943
The Act was passed to address the above problems where a contract is discharged by frustration.

The main provisions of the Act are as follows:

1 Recovery of money paid.

> **LEGISLATION HIGHLIGHTER**
>
> Section 1(2) of the 1943 Act provides that money paid before the frustrating event is recoverable and money payable before the frustrating event ceases to be payable, whether or not there has been a total failure of consideration.
>
> If, however, the party to whom such sums are paid or are payable incurred expenses before discharge in performance of the contract, the court may award him or her such expenses up to the limit of the money paid or payable before the frustrating event.
>
> It follows that if nothing was paid or payable before discharge, they will be unable to recover expenses, although they may be able to rely on s.1(3) below.

In *Gamerco SA v ICM/Fair Warning (Agency) Ltd*, 1995, Garland J said that in calculating the award under s.1(2), there was:

> "no indication in the [Act], the authorities or relevant literature that the court is obliged to incline towards total retention or equal division. Its task is to do justice in a situation which the parties had neither contemplated nor provided for, and to mitigate the possible harshness of allowing all loss to lie where it falls."

2 Valuable benefit.

LEGISLATION HIGHLIGHTER

Section 1(3) of the 1943 Act provides that if one party has, by reason of anything done by the other party in performance of the contract, obtained a valuable benefit (other than money) before the frustrating event, they may be ordered to pay a just sum in respect of it. In arriving at the sum, the court must consider all the circumstances of the case, in particular whether the benefited party has incurred expenses in the performance of the contract before the time of discharge and the effect, in relation to the benefit, of the circumstances giving rise to the frustration of the contract. Any sums retained or recovered by the other party under s.1(2) may also be taken into account.

It is likely that s.1(3) was enacted with *Appleby v Myers*, 1867, in mind. In that case, the claimants agreed to install machinery in the defendant's factory for £459. When the work was nearly completed, an accidental fire destroyed the factory and all its contents. An action for £419 for work and materials failed; the contract was frustrated and no payment was due at the time of discharge.

In fact, it may be doubted whether *Appleby v Myers* would be decided any differently even after the Act of 1943, particularly if the court were to take a narrow view of the meaning of "valuable benefit". This would seem to be confirmed by *B.P. Exploration Co (Libya) v Hunt (No.2)*, 1979, affirmed HL, 1983, where Robert Goff J said:

> "where the services rendered by the [claimant] have an end-product, s.1(3) shows that the value of the end-product is the benefit. Where a contract is frustrated by a fire which destroys a building on which work has been done, the award will be nil."

3 Scope of the Act.

There are certain contracts to which the Act does not apply, including the following:

(1) any charter party, except time charters and charters by way of demise, or any other contract for the carriage of goods by sea;

(2) contracts of insurance; and

(3) contracts for the sale of specific goods which are frustrated by the goods perishing.

BREACH

A breach of contract will occur where one party fails to fulfil, or intimates that they do not intend to fulfil, their obligations under the contract.

The consequences of the breach of particular types of term has already been considered (see Chapter 6), but for present purposes it should be noted that some breaches entitle the innocent party to sue for damages only; others, more serious, entitle the innocent party, in addition to claiming damages, to treat themselves as discharged from the contract. Serious breaches of this nature are generally described as "repudiatory" breaches. After such a breach, the innocent party has an election; they may decide to accept the breach as a repudiation of the contract or may decide to affirm the contract, i.e. the innocent party is not bound to discharge themselves from the contract. Where they decide to treat the breach as repudiatory, this state of affairs must be communicated to the other party. This communication requires no particular form, "the aggrieved party need not personally ... notify the repudiating party of his election ... it is sufficient that the fact of the election comes to the repudiating party's attention" (per Lord Steyn in *Vitol S.A. v Norelf Ltd*, HL, 1996).

In order to establish that a breach of contract amounts to a repudiation, it must be shown that the contract-breaking party has, beyond reasonable doubt, evinced an intention no longer to fulfil his or her part of the contract; *Woodar Investment Developments Ltd v Wimpey Construction UK Ltd*, HL, 1980.

Anticipatory Breach

A breach may occur before performance is due, i.e. where the party effectively intimates that they do not intend to perform their part of the contract. In such a case, the breach is described as an "anticipatory breach". Anticipatory breach may be explicit, as in *Hochster v De La Tour*, 1853, where the defendant agreed in April to employ the claimant as a courier commencing June. In May, the defendant informed the claimant that he would not require his services. The claimant's action for damages in May succeeded. Alternatively, it may be implicit, where the defendant by conduct disables themselves from performance, as in *Frost v Knight*, 1870. Here, the defendant, having agreed to marry the claimant on his father's death, broke off the engagement during the father's lifetime. It was held that the claimant was at that point entitled to damages.

In both cases, the innocent party has an immediate right of action; they may sue for breach of contract at once (i.e. the innocent party may "accept the repudiation") or they may await the date of performance and hold the other party to the contract. Where the innocent party refuses to accept the repudiation, the contract remains in force and the rights of the innocent party are preserved. The possible consequences of this are illustrated by *White and Carter (Councils) Ltd v McGregor*, HL, 1962 (see Chapter 14).

Refusing to accept a repudiation is not without its risks as the innocent party may lose their right of action if the contract becomes frustrated in the intervening period before performance is due; *Avery v Bowden*, 1855.

. . . .

AGREEMENT

A contract may be discharged or varied by agreement. As a general rule, consideration will be required to render an agreement to discharge or vary valid, and in some cases formalities will be required.

Consideration and Formalities

Where a simple contract is executory on both sides, an agreement to discharge or vary the contract provides its own consideration; each party agrees to release the other from his or her outstanding obligations under the contract.

Where a simple contract is executed on one side, a deed is required to effect a valid release of the other party. In the absence of a deed, the other party must provide new consideration (an "accord and satisfaction"). The consideration itself need not be executed but may consist of an executory promise; *Elton Cop Dyeing Co v Broadbent and Son Ltd*, CA, 1919. The same principles apply to a variation.

There are two special cases:

(1) Contracts required to be evidenced in writing. Where the contract requires written evidence to be enforceable (see Chapter 5), the contract may be validly discharged by an oral agreement, with no requirement of written evidence; *Morris v Baron*, 1918. Although the oral words suffice to discharge the original agreement, any new agreement substituted in its place will require written evidence, as will any variation of the original agreement.

(2) Contracts by deed. At common law, a contract by deed could only be discharged in the form in which it was made. However, in equity (which now prevails), such a contract may be validly discharged or varied by an oral agreement; *Berry v Berry*, 1929.

PERFORMANCE

If both parties perform their obligations under the contract, the contract is discharged. This raises the question, what amounts to performance?

The general rule is that performance must be precise and exact. Thus, in one case, the defendants agreed to buy from the claimants 3,000 tins of tinned fruit to be packed in cases containing 30 tins. Some of the consignment was packed in cases containing 24 tins and it was held that the defendants were entitled to reject the whole consignment; *Re Moore Co and Landauer Co*, 1921 (criticised in *Reardon Smith Line Ltd v Hansen-Tangen*, HL, 1976). It should be noted, however, that s.15A of the Sale of Goods Act 1979 prevents the purchaser from unreasonably rejecting goods which are only slightly different from the contract description, subject to any contrary provisions in the contract. The hardship of the precise performance rule is illustrated by *Cutter v Powell*, 1795, where a seaman, having agreed to serve on a ship from Jamaica to Liverpool for 30 guineas payable on completion of the voyage, died in mid-voyage. The contract was construed to be "entire" and therefore his widow could recover nothing in respect of the work done.

The harshness of the general rule is mitigated by various exceptions:

1 Severable contracts
"Entire" contracts tend to be the exception rather than the rule. A contract will be "severable" where some of the obligations in the contract may be enforced independently of performance by the other party.

Whether obligations are entire or severable is a question of construction; the tendency in contracts for work and materials is towards severability. Thus, in *Roberts v Havelock*, 1832, a ship en route was damaged and had to be docked for essential repairs. The claimant carried out the repairs, but before he had completed the contract, he requested payment for work done thus far. His action succeeded as the contract did not require him to complete all the repairs before he made a demand for payment.

2 Substantial performance
A party who performs his contractual obligations substantially though not precisely, may enforce the contract; *Boone v Eyre*, 1779. However, the substantial performer may himself be liable for damages in respect of his partial performance. Two cases illustrate the operation of the doctrine.

DAKIN CO LTD V LEE, CA, 1916
The claimant builders agreed to carry out repairs to the defendant's house. The work as carried out departed from the specification in three minor respects which could be remedied at a relatively small cost.

Held: Judgment would be given for the claimant, subject to a deduction equal to the cost of remedying the defects.

Comment
By way of comparison, in *Bolton v Mahadeva*, CA, 1972, the claimant agreed to install central heating in the defendant's house for £560. The system was defective in that the house was not heated adequately and noxious fumes were given off inside the house. The cost of remedying the defects was £174. The court held that there had not been substantial performance and the claimant was not entitled to recover anything.

In order to rely on the doctrine of substantial performance, the claimant's breach must amount only to a breach of warranty, or a non-serious breach of an innominate term. Where a condition has been broken, the doctrine cannot be relied on.

Voluntary Acceptance of Partial Performance
Where performance by one party is only partial, the other party may accept the partial performance; *Christy v Row*, 1808. Implicit in the idea of acceptance of partial performance is the notion that the parties have effectively entered into a fresh agreement.

Where partial performance is accepted, the partial performer may have a claim on a quantum meruit basis in respect of work done (see Chapter 14).

The other party must have a genuine choice whether or not to accept the partial performance. In *Sumpter v Hedges*, CA, 1898, the claimant agreed to erect buildings on the defendant's land. He did about two-thirds of the work and then abandoned the contract, leaving the defendant himself to complete the buildings. The claimant's action on quantum meruit failed; the defendant had no choice whether to accept or reject the partial performance.

Prevention of Performance by Breach or Frustration
A party may be wrongfully prevented by the other party from completing performance. The injured party in such a situation may claim damages for breach of contract or claim on a quantum meruit for the work done; *Planche v Colburn*, 1831.

Alternatively, if the contract is frustrated, it is automatically discharged and the parties excused further performance.

TENDER OF PERFORMANCE

Where one party is unable to complete performance without the collaboration of the other party, they may make an offer or "tender" of performance which is rejected by the other party. If this is the case, the party tendering performance will be discharged from further liability. Thus, a tender of performance is equivalent to performance.

In *Startup v Macdonald*, 1843, the claimant, having agreed to deliver oil within the last 14 days of March, tried to deliver it at 8.30pm on the last day of that month, but the defendant refused to take delivery. The claimant's action for damages succeeded.

However, s.29(5) of the Sale of Goods Act 1979 enacts that a tender of goods must be made at a reasonable hour; what is reasonable is a question of fact.

Where a party is under a contractual obligation to pay a sum of money, a tender of money by that party, if refused by the other party, will not discharge the tenderer from liability. If sued, the tenderer may pay the sum of money into court and if the action is proceeded with, the other party may be ordered to pay costs.

STIPULATIONS AS TO TIME

Where the contract does not fix a time for performance, as a general rule performance must be effected within a reasonable time. This is given statutory effect by s.29(3) of the Sale of Goods Act 1979 in relation to the obligation to deliver the goods under a contract of sale.

At common law, where a time was fixed for performance of one party's obligations under the contract, time was "of the essence". The failure to perform by the appointed date amounted to a breach of contract entitling the innocent party to treat themselves as discharged. Nevertheless, equity would grant specific performance despite a failure to comply with a stipulation as to time, and s.41 of the Law of Property Act 1925 (re-enacting s.25 of the Judicature Act 1873) provides that the equitable principle shall prevail.

The result is that time is not of the essence where a contract fixes a date for performance unless it falls under one of the following exceptional cases:

(1) where the contract expressly provides that time is of the essence;

(2) where the contract was not originally one where time was of the essence, but it is made of the essence by a party subjected to unreasonable delay giving notice to the other party to perform within a reasonable time;

(3) where it must be inferred from the nature of the subject-matter and the circumstances surrounding the contract that time is of the essence.

Where time is of the essence in a contract, it is clear that any delay, however slight, will amount to repudiation; *Union Eagle Ltd v Golden Achievement Ltd*, PC, 1997.

Where time is not of the essence, the failure to perform by the stipulated time is still nevertheless a breach of contract entitling the injured party to damages; *Raineri v Miles*, HL, 1980.

REVISION CHECKLIST

You should now know and understand:

☐ **how a contract becomes discharged by frustration and the effects of frustration;**

☐ **how the** Law Reform (Frustrated Contracts) Act 1943 **deals with the effects of frustration;**

☐ **the circumstances in which a contract becomes discharged by breach and the consequences;**

☐ **the ways in which a contract may be discharged by agreement;**

☐ **how discharge by performance occurs and the exceptions to the rule of precise performance.**

QUESTION AND ANSWER

THE QUESTION

Mike was the proprietor of the Bona Vista Hotel in Whitepool, a seaside resort. The local council organised a week-long tennis tournament in Whitepool. The Sherwood Tennis Club ("S"), based 200 miles away, booked the hotel for the exclusive use of its members for the duration of the tournament for a total sum of £5,000.

S sent Mike a deposit of £1,000 in advance, with the balance to be paid on S's departure at the end of the stay. Mike incurred expenditure if £1,400 on additional catering facilities in preparation for the visit.

Shortly before the tournament was due to commence, an accidental fire destroyed the sports complex where it was to be held and no suitable alternative venue could be arranged in time. The tournament was cancelled. As a result of that, S cancelled the booking and Mike was unable to re-let the rooms.

Mike also engaged Barry, a builder, to construct a new extension to the hotel. The price for the job was fixed at £100,000 payable on completion. When the work was nearly completed, a fire totally destroyed the extension.

Barry is now claiming £90,000 for work done and materials provided.

Advise Mike of his legal position in relation to S and Barry.

ADVICE AND THE ANSWER

General guidance
The question is concerned with discharge by frustration. Problem questions on this topic usually involve a two-stage process. First, one may have to consider whether the contract is frustrated; and secondly, there is the issue of the legal consequences of frustration. The difficulty here is that, at common law, the contract is discharged from the moment of frustration onwards. The effects of this can operate vary harshly and as a result, the Law Reform (Frustrated Contracts) Act 1943 was passed. Those candidates who handle the provisions of the Act best tend to get a good mark on frustration questions. However, it is not a particularly well drafted measure and there are uncertainties as to its application. The following plan demonstrates how the answer should be structured.

Answer plan
1 The answer should begin by defining frustration, i.e. discharge will occur if, during the currency of the contract the objective that the parties had in view becomes impossible to achieve owing to a fundamental change of circumstances that is outside their control.
2 The dictum of Lord Radcliffe in *Davis Contractors Ltd v Fareham UDC*, HL, 1956, may be quoted, i.e. that it is not hardship, inconvenience or material loss which calls frustration into play, "there must be as well a change in the significance of the obligation that the thing undertaken would, if performed, be a different thing from that contracted for".

3 Is the contract between Mike and S frustrated? Does the non-occurrence of the tennis tournament frustrate the contract? Position depends upon whether the tournament is the "foundation" of the contract—test laid down in *Krell v Henry*, CA, 1903. That case should be discussed and compared with *Herne Bay Steam Boat Co v Hutton*, CA, 1903.

4 The distinction between the contracting party's personal *motive* and the *object* of contract should be explained. Factors indicating that the tournament may lie at the foundation include the fact that S is a tennis club, and that it has booked the hotel for the exclusive use of its members for the duration of the tournament.

5 If the contract between Mike and S is frustrated, can S recover its deposit of £1,000? At common law, the loss lay were it fell; *Chandler v Webster*, CA, 1904. The position was modified by the House of Lords in the *Fibrosa* case to allow recovery where there had been a total failure of consideration. Under the Law Reform (Frustrated Contracts) Act 1943 s.1(2), S may in principle recover money paid before frustration subject to the court's discretion to award Mike expenses up to, but not exceeding, the amount paid or payable before frustration. Court not obliged to incline towards total retention or equal division; *Gamerco SA v ICM/Fair Warning (Agency) Ltd*, 1995.

6 Is the contract between Mike and Barry frustrated? Assuming the fire is not the fault of Barry, the contract may be discharged; *Taylor v Caldwell*, HL, 1863. At common law, Barry would have recovered nothing as loss lay where it fell; *Appleby v Myers*, 1867.

7 Under the Law Reform (Frustrated Contracts) Act 1943, s.1(3), Barry may, at the court's discretion, recover a just sum for conferring a valuable benefit on Mike by virtue of anything done by Barry in performance of the contract before the time of discharge. However, in *B.P. Exploration Co (Libya) v Hunt (No.2)*, HL, 1983, there was a suggestion that the valuable benefit should be the end-product of the service and not just the service itself. If this is the case, Barry may recover nothing as the works have been totally destroyed and no award can be made on a quantum meruit basis.

Remedies

INTRODUCTION

In this chapter, we examine the various remedies for breach of contract. Where a party suffers loss as a result of a breach of contract, they may be entitled to:

1 An award of damages
2 As an alternative, bring a claim on a "quantum meruit" for work partially completed under the contract
3 In an appropriate case, the equitable remedy of specific performance
4 In an appropriate case, the equitable remedy of injunction

These remedies will be considered below.

DAMAGES

Basis of the Award

> **CHECKPOINT**
>
> "Expectation loss"—such damages are normally awarded on the basis of placing the injured party in the same financial position as if the contract had been properly performed, i.e. compensation for "loss of bargain" or loss of expectations under the contract. This is the standard basis for the award of damages in contract.
> "Reliance loss"—such damages are awarded to compensate the claimant for expenses incurred in reliance on the contract which have been wasted by the defendant's breach. Such awards tend to be the exception rather than the rule.

Where damages are awarded on the reliance basis, it seems that pre-contractual expenses may be included. In *Anglia Television Ltd v Reed*, CA, 1971, the claimants engaged the defendant, an actor, to play a part in a film. Before this, the claimants had incurred expenditure in employing a director and a designer. The defendant repudiated the contract and it was held that the claimants were entitled to recover their wasted expenditure. However, in

C. and P. Haulage v Middleton, CA, 1983, the Court of Appeal awarded only nominal damages on the reliance basis as the bargain the claimant had entered into turned out to be a bad one for him; i.e. the expenditure was not wasted by the defendant's breach.

In the *Anglia Television* case (above), it seems to have been assumed that the film, if made, would have made enough money to at least cover the claimant's expenditure. In *C.C.C. Films (London) Ltd v Impact Quadrant Films Ltd*, 1984, a case not dissimilar on the facts, it was held that the burden lay on the defendant to show that the transaction was so unprofitable as to not even cover the claimant's expenses.

In *Omak Maritime Ltd v Mamola Challenger Shipping Co*, 2010, it was held that a claim for lost profits and a claim for wasted expenditure should not be treated as independent claims that could not be "mixed". Both claims were governed by a principle which required a comparison between the claimant's current position and what it would have been had the contract been performed; thus damages for reliance loss are best explained as a species of expectation loss.

Restitutionary Damages

There is a third basis on which damages for breach of contract are awarded, and that is the restitutionary interest. It seems that in a suitable case, damages can be measured by the benefit gained by the wrongdoer from the breach; *Wrotham Park Estate Co Ltd v Parkside Homes Ltd*, 1974. This principle was applied in unusual circumstances in *Attorney-General v Blake*, HL, 2000. Blake, a British intelligence officer, had spied for the Soviet Union and was convicted and imprisoned for treason. He escaped and defected to Moscow where he wrote an autobiography which was published in England. Publication was a breach of Blake's former contract of employment. An injunction was granted preventing payment of the royalties to Blake.

There are, however, limits to the application of this principle. In *Experience Hendrix v PPX Enterprises*, CA, 2003, an action was brought to compel a company who had released some unlicensed recordings of guitarist Jimi Hendrix's music to provide a full account of profits. The Court of Appeal held that the case was not sufficiently exceptional in that, unlike *Blake*, it did not involve national security nor was there any element of a fiduciary obligation. The court held that the defendants should pay the claimants merely a reasonable sum for their use of the recordings.

Damages are also awarded on the restitutionary basis where a purchaser recovers an advance payment for goods that the seller, in breach of contract, fails to deliver. In an appropriate case, a claim for expectation loss may be combined with a claim for reliance loss; and a restitutionary claim can be joined with one for expectation or reliance loss. In fact, there is nothing to prevent all three interests being recovered, in an appropriate case; *Millar's Machinery Co v David Way & Son*, 1935.

Contributory Negligence

Although it is clear that contractual liability may be removed altogether by the claimant's fault (*Quinn v Burch Bros (Builders) Ltd*, 1966), the law has been less clear whether damages for breach of contract can be apportioned by the court on the ground of the claimant's contributory negligence under the Law Reform (Contributory Negligence) Act 1945.

The law has been clarified as a result of *Forsikringsaktieselskapet Vesta v Butcher*, CA, 1988. Where the defendant's liability in contract is the same as his liability in the tort of negligence independently of the existence of any contract, the defendant may raise the defence of contributory negligence whether the action is brought in contract or tort. However, where contractual liability is strict the Act of 1945 does not apply; *Barclays Bank v Fairclough Building Ltd*, CA, 1994.

Damages for Mental Distress

Although damages in contract may be recovered for physical inconvenience and pain and suffering caused by personal injury, it was always thought that damages could not generally be recovered for mental distress; *Addis v Gramophone Co Ltd*, HL, 1909. Here, the House of Lords refused to award damages for injury to feelings in a wrongful dismissal case. However, where the mental distress results from an employer's breach of an implied term concerning trust and confidence, there is no reason in principle why such damages should not be awarded; *Johnson v Unisys Ltd*, HL, 2001. Where the contract is for a holiday, recreation or entertainment, it is clear that substantial damages may be recoverable for disappointment, vexation and mental distress; *Jarvis v Swann Tours*, CA, 1973.

Despite some earlier cases which seemed to call into question the Addis principle, it seems to have been confirmed, at least in relation to contracts of employment; *Bliss v South East Thames Regional Health Authority*, CA, 1985. A similar approach was taken by the Court of Appeal in relation to a contract to buy a house in *Watts v Morrow*, CA, 1991. This case was distinguished in *Farley v Skinner (No.2)*, HL, 2001, where a homebuyer employed a surveyor to investigate whether a country house was affected by aircraft noise. It was held that the claimant was entitled, in principle, to recover non-pecuniary damages for distress and inconvenience resulting from the surveyor's negligence. The House of Lords considered that, in future, it will be "sufficient if a major or important object of the contract is to give pleasure, relaxation or piece of mind". However, the damages awarded by the courts under this head should be modest—in *Farley v Skinner* the sum of £10,000 was awarded.

Remoteness of Damage

The claimant may not be able to recover damages for all the loss they have suffered as some of the loss may be adjudged by the court to be too remote a consequence of the breach to be eligible for compensation by the defendant. The rules concerning remoteness of damage in contract were originally laid down in the following case.

KEY CASE

HADLEY V BAXENDALE, HL, 1854

The claimants were millers who contracted with the defendant carriers to take a broken mill shaft to the repairers, as a pattern for a new shaft. The claimants had no spare shaft. Although the defendants had promised to deliver within a day, they in fact delayed, and the shaft was not delivered until a week later. The claimants sued the defendants for damages for loss of profits arising from the fact that the mill was out of action for longer than anticipated, owing to the delay.

Held: The defendants were not liable for the loss of profits—the loss was too remote. Alderson B. said that damages for breach of contract "should be such as may fairly and reasonably be considered either arising naturally, i.e. according to the usual course of things, from such breach of contract itself, or such as may reasonably be supposed to have been in the contemplation of both parties, at the time they made the contract, as the probable result of the breach of it".

Comment

In this case, the claimant's loss did not arise "naturally" because the claimants might well have possessed a spare shaft; neither was it "in the contemplation of the parties", as the defendants were unaware that the shaft entrusted to them was the only one which the claimants possessed.

The principle laid down in *Hadley v Baxendale* was restated by the Court of Appeal in *Victoria Laundry (Windsor) Ltd v Newman Industries Ltd*, CA, 1949 and discussed by the House of Lords in *The Heron II*, HL, 1969. As a result of these cases, remoteness of damage may be divided into two sub- rules, one of which must be satisfied if a particular head of damage is not to be adjudged too remote. Thus, the claimant may recover for:

(1) loss arising naturally out of the breach, i.e. in the ordinary course of

things. As a reasonable person, the contract-breaking party is taken to know what this loss will be; or

(2) (in relation to special, abnormal or unusual loss) loss which could reasonably be supposed to have been within the contemplation of the parties, at the time of the contract, as the probable result of the breach.

Further, the courts have held that provided a particular type of loss is within the reasonable contemplation of the parties, the loss will not be too remote if its extent was far more serious than could have been reasonably contemplated; *H. Parsons (Livestock) Ltd v Uttley Ingham Co Ltd*, CA, 1978; *Brown v K. M. R. Services Ltd*, CA, 1995.

A classic illustration of the workings of the remoteness rules is afforded by the *Victoria Laundry* case. The claimants, launderers and dyers, wished to acquire another boiler to enable them to expand their business and to take on certain lucrative dyeing contracts. The defendants agreed to sell to the claimants a boiler which, as the defendants were aware, was required for immediate use. Delivery was five months late and the claimants claimed loss of profits as follows:

(1) £16 per week representing loss of "normal" profits representing the additional custom they would have taken on; and

(2) £262 per week representing the loss of the lucrative dyeing contracts.

The Court of Appeal held that the defendants' state of knowledge made them liable for (1), but not (2), about which they neither knew nor could be taken to know. A similar approach was taken in *Balfour Beatty Construction (Scotland) Ltd v Scottish Power Plc*, HL, 1994, where it was held that there was no general principle that parties were presumed to have knowledge of each other's business practices, especially where complex construction or manufacturing processes were involved.

The operation of the rule in *Hadley v Baxendale* was reviewed by the House of Lords in *Transfield Shipping Inc v Mercator Shipping Inc*, HL, 2008. Two members of the court (Lords Hoffmann and Hope) adopted a formulation of the remoteness test different from that laid down in the traditional line of cases. This involved asking whether the contract-breaker could reasonably be regarded as assuming responsibility for the losses in question at the time of the agreement. Under this approach, the question to be asked is, not merely whether the parties must be taken to have had the particular type of loss within their contemplation at the time of the contract, but also whether they had *liability* for this type of loss within their contemplation. This question involved the interpretation of the contract as a whole against its commercial background.

It is doubtful whether *Transfield v Mercator* has introduced a new general test for remoteness of damage in contract law. In *Sylvia Shipping Co Ltd v Progress Bulk Carriers Ltd*, 2010, the court considered that the traditional approach remains the general test of remoteness in the great majority of cases. There may be rare or unusual cases where it may be necessary to consider whether there had been an assumption of responsibility; this would be where the application of the general test leads to a disproportionate liability or would be contrary to market understanding and expectations. In those unusual cases where the assumption of responsibility test is applicable, if the loss is within the scope of the test, it will not be too remote even if it would not have occurred in ordinary circumstances; *Supershield Ltd v Siemens Building Technologies FE Ltd*, CA, 2010.

That the time of the contract is the relevant time for determining whether the loss is too remote was confirmed by the House of Lords in *Jackson v Royal Bank of Scotland*, HL, 2005.

Figure 26: Damages for Breach of Contract

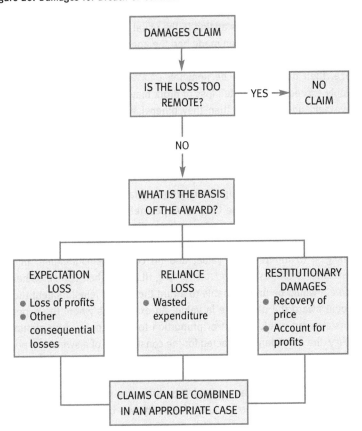

Measure of Damages

Once it is established that loss is not too remote, the next question is the measure of damages, i.e. how is the loss to be quantified? The normal rule is that damages are assessed as at the date of the acceptance of repudiation, however in exceptional cases subsequent events may be taken into account: *The Golden Victory*, HL, 2007.

There are no specific rules for the quantification of damages in contract; quantification is a matter for the court. One exception concerns contracts for the sale of goods. Section 51 of the Sale of Goods Act 1979 provides that where the seller fails to deliver the goods and the buyer brings an action for non-delivery, where there is an available market for the goods, the measure of damages should be the difference between the contract price and the current market price at the time when the goods ought to have been delivered.

Similarly, where the buyer refuses to accept or pay for the goods, s.50 provides that where there is an available market, the measure of damages should be the difference between the contract price and the current market price at the time when the goods ought to have been accepted. Where the seller is a dealer, the loss arising in the usual course of things is the loss of profit that would have been made had the goods been sold to that particular buyer. If they have been able to find another buyer at the same or higher price, their damages will be nominal; *Charter v Sullivan*, CA, 1957. Where supply exceeds demand, full loss of profit may be awarded as the dealer will have sold one less item than they otherwise would; *W.L. Thompson Ltd v Robinson (Gunmakers) Ltd*, 1955.

In any type of contract, the fact that an award of damages involves an element of speculation will not prevent the award being made. In *Chaplin v Hicks*, CA, 1911, the claimant recovered substantial damages against the organiser of a beauty competition, who had failed, in breach of contract, to invite her for interview. The Court of Appeal refused to upset the award even though the claimant was by no means certain to have been successful.

It seems that in building contracts, there are two principal measures of damages, (i) difference in value; and (ii) cost of reinstatement. In *Ruxley Electronics and Construction Ltd v Forsyth*, HL, 1995, their Lordships held that where it would be unreasonable to award the cost of reinstatement the court should award the difference in value. An example is where the expense of reinstatement would be out of proportion to the benefit to be obtained. In *Ruxley*, the defendant contracted for the construction of a swimming pool of a maximum depth of 7ft 6in, but on completion the pool was only 6ft 9in deep. As the pool was perfectly serviceable it was held that the appropriate measure was the difference in value. This difference was nil although the trial judge's award of £2,500 for loss of amenity was upheld. The cost of reconstruction would have amounted to over £20,000.

Mitigation

There is an expectation on the claimant to take all reasonable steps to mitigate the loss caused by the breach of contract.

Recovery cannot be made for any part of the loss which the defendant can prove to have resulted from a failure to mitigate; *British Westinghouse Electric Co v Underground Electric Railway Co of London*, HL, 1912.

In *Brace v Calder*, 1895, the defendants were a four-member partnership who agreed to employ the claimant as manager for two years. Shortly after, the partnership was dissolved which amounted to wrongful dismissal of the claimant. Then two of the former partners offered to employ the claimant on the same terms but he refused the offer. The claimant brought an action to recover the salary he would have received had he served the full two years. It was held that he was entitled only to nominal damages as it was unreasonable to have rejected the offer of continued employment.

The claimant is only required to act reasonably; they would not be required, in order to mitigate, to embark on a hazardous or uncertain course of action; *Pilkington v Wood*, 1953. Further, if, on an anticipatory breach (see Chapter 13), the injured party elects to affirm the contract instead of accepting the repudiation, they will be under no duty to mitigate before the date due for performance.

Liquidated Damages and Penalties

> **CHECKPOINT**
>
> "Liquidated damages"—a contractual clause providing for the payment of a fixed sum on breach. If the sum represents a genuine pre-estimate of the loss, the court will allow the claimant, on breach, to recover this sum without proof of actual loss. This is so whether the actual loss is greater or smaller than the sum stipulated in the contract. Such provisions are sometimes also referred to as "agreed damages" clauses.
>
> "Penalty"—where the sum stipulated in the contract is not a genuine pre-estimate of the loss, but is more in the nature of a threat held over the head of the other party to compel performance, it is referred to as a "penalty". A penalty is invalid and a claimant who attempts to enforce a penalty may recover compensation only for their actual loss.

In the unlikely event that the loss exceeds the sum stipulated in the penalty clause, the claimant may elect to recover his or her full loss; this option does not exist in the case of liquidated damages. Whether a clause is a liquidated damages clause or a penalty is a question of construction depending upon the intention of the parties judged as at the time the contract was made. Rules for the guidance of the courts were laid down in the following case.

KEY CASE

DUNLOP PNEUMATIC TYRE CO LTD V NEW GARAGE AND MOTOR CO LTD, HL, 1915:
The claimants supplied tyres to the defendants subject to an agreement that the defendants would not, inter alia, resell them below list price. The defendants had to pay £5 "by way of liquidated damages and not as a penalty" for every tyre sold in breach of the agreement. The question arose as to the nature of the clause—liquidated damages or penalty?

Held: The provision was not penal and was in the nature of liquidated damages. The following rules for the guidance of the court were laid down:
(1) The expression used by the parties to describe the sum is a relevant, but not a conclusive, factor; e.g. it may be described as "agreed damages" but in fact be a penalty, and vice versa.
(2) If the sum stipulated for is extravagant and unconscionable in relation to the greatest loss which could conceivably follow the breach, it will be a penalty.
(3) Where the breach consists of the non-payment of a sum of money and the sum to be paid on breach is greater than the sum which ought to have been paid, the sum is a penalty.
(4) There is a presumption (but no more) that where a single lump sum is to be paid on the occurrence of one or more or all of several events, some serious and others not, the lump sum is a penalty.
(5) A sum is not prevented from being liquidated damages by the fact that precise pre-estimation of the loss is impossible.

Comment
Undercutting on price would certainly have damaged the claimants' business, and though precise pre-estimation of the loss was impossible, the sum stipulated for here was reasonable in the circumstances and not in the nature of a penalty.

Sometimes a contract may stipulate for a sum of money to be paid upon the occurrence of an event that is not a breach of contract, as in *Alder v Moore*, 1961. The House of Lords have confirmed, in *Export Credit Guarantee Department v Universal Oil Products Co*, HL, 1983, that the penalty rules (set out above) only apply to sums of money payable on breach. But in *Jobson v*

Johnson, CA, 1988, the court held that the equitable rules against contractual penalty clauses applied where the penalty involved the transfer of property whose value exceeded the actual loss of the innocent party, as well as where it involved the payment of an excessive sum of money.

ACTION FOR AN AGREED SUM

An action for damages in contract as discussed above must be distinguished from an action for an agreed sum, such as an agreed price for work and materials or the price of goods sold. In an action for an agreed sum, the issues of remoteness and measures of damages (as discussed above) do not arise, although the action will not be available if damages are in fact an adequate remedy. There is, however, an exception to this last point; i.e. where the situation in the following case arises.

KEY CASE

WHITE AND CARTER (COUNCILS) LTD V MCGREGOR, HL, 1962
The appellants agreed to advertise the respondents' business on litter bins for a period of three years at an agreed price. The respondents repudiated the contract the very day it was made but the appellants chose to ignore the repudiation and displayed the advertisements for three years, eventually claiming the full amount due under the contract.

Held: The appellants were entitled to recover the amount agreed under the contract.

Comment
There has been some controversy concerning this decision and it is subject to certain limitations set out below.
(1) the *White and Carter* principle will not apply where the co-operation of the other party is required, such as where work under the contract is carried out on the defendant's land, as in *Hounslow LPC v Twickenham Garden Developments Ltd*, 1971;
(2) it may not apply where the claimant has no legitimate financial or other interest in performing the contract rather than claiming damages, such as business commitments with third parties. The legitimate interest factor was allowed in *The Odenfeld*, 1978 and rejected in *Clea Shipping Corp v Bulk Oil International Ltd*, 1984; and
(3) a further limitation is suggested by *Attica Sea Carriers Corp v Ferrostaal Poseidon Buld Reederei GmbH*, CA, 1976, where Lord Denning

MR was of the view that a party cannot rely on the *White and Carter* principle where they ought in all reason to accept the other party's repudiation and sue for damages immediately. This was confirmed in *Isabella Shipowner SA v Shagang Shipping Co Ltd*, 2012 where it was held that affirmation had to be "extremely unreasonable" or "perverse" before there was no legitimate interest in performing the contract.

QUANTUM MERUIT

A claim on a quantum meruit ("as much as he deserves") is a claim for reasonable remuneration. The remedy is distinct from an award of damages which is essentially compensation for loss. A claim on a quantum meruit may arise where one party is prevented by the other (in breach), from completing performance. The injured party may claim on a quantum meruit; *Planche v Colburn*, 1831. In this situation, the remedy is available as an alternative to claiming damages. Similarly, a claim may arise where a partial performance is voluntarily accepted by the other party; the partial performer may sue on a (see under "Discharge by Performance", Chapter 13).

SPECIFIC PERFORMANCE AND INJUNCTION

Specific performance and injunction are equitable remedies, not available as of right but at the discretion of the court (cf. damages). The remedies will only be granted where it is equitable to do so, and may be refused on the ground of hardship.

Specific Performance

Specific performance is an order of the court compelling the defendant to perform their part of the contract. The court has power to award damages in addition to, or instead of, specific performance (or an injunction). The fact that the remedy may be refused on the ground of hardship is illustrated by *Patel v Ali*, 1984. Specific performance was refused of a contract for the sale of a house, as the defendant vendor, who spoke little English, had contracted a serious illness and needed to be near friends and relatives. The claimant was left to the common law remedy of damages on the ground that exceptional hardship would result if specific performance was granted.

The remedy is subject to certain limitations:

(1) Damages inadequate: Specific performance will only be granted where

damages are an inadequate remedy. Thus, it will not, in general, be awarded of a contract for the sale of goods (*Cohen› v Roche*, 1927), although the power to award it is contained in s.52 of the Sale of Goods Act 1979.

Specific performance is most commonly ordered in relation to the breach of contract for the sale of land, since, land being unique, damages will not usually be adequate compensation. In *Beswick v Beswick*, HL, 1968, the remedy was granted to enforce a contractual obligation to pay a sum of money (see Chapter 12).

(2) Contracts requiring constant supervision: Specific performance will not be granted where the constant supervision of the court would be required, e.g. where a contract required a resident porter to be in attendance at a block of flats, the remedy was refused; *Ryan v Mutual Tontine Westminster Chambers Association*, CA, 1893. The principle was applied to a covenant in a commercial lease in *Co-operative Insurance Ltd v Argyll Stores (Holdings) Ltd*, HL, 1997.

(3) Contracts for personal services: Specific performance will not be awarded where the contract involves personal services, e.g. a contract of employment.

(4) Lack of mutuality: Specific performance will not, in general, be ordered against a defendant unless the remedy could have been ordered against the claimant, e.g. a claimant who is a minor; *Flight v Bolland*, 1828. Mutuality is normally considered as at the time of the judgment rather than the time when the contract was made; *Price v Strange*, CA, 1977.

Injunction

An injunction may be granted to restrain a breach of negative stipulation (a promise not to do something) in a contract.

There is a general principle that an injunction will not be granted if its effect would be to compel a party to a contract to do something which could not have been made subject to an order of specific performance, e.g. to require performance of a contract for personal services. In *Page One Records Ltd v Britton*, 1968, the manager of the pop group The Troggs sought an injunction restraining them from appointing, in breach of contract, anyone else as manager. The injunction was refused on the ground that, if granted, its effect would be to compel performance of a personal services contract. Very exceptionally an injunction may be granted in these circumstances, for example, where an employee is dismissed in breach of contract as a result of trade union pressure; *Hill v CA Parsons Co Ltd*, CA, 1972.

An injunction may be granted to restrain a breach of a negative stipulation in a personal services contract providing it does not actually compel performance. In *Warner Bros Pictures Inc v Nelson*, 1937, the actress Bette Davis agreed with the claimants not to act for any other film company for a year; during that period she did work for another company. An injunction was granted restraining her from so doing; the effect of the injunction was to encourage, rather than compel, performance since she would be free to earn her living in some way other than acting.

REVISION CHECKLIST

You should now know and understand:

- ☐ the principles relating to an award of damages for breach of contract;
- ☐ the circumstances in which a quantum meruit may be awarded;
- ☐ the principles relating to the equitable remedy of injunction;
- ☐ the principles relating to the equitable remedy of specific performance.

QUESTION AND ANSWER

THE QUESTION

Millicent owns a factory manufacturing clothing. In January, the heating system of the factory broke down and she was forced to lay off the workforce. Millicent engaged Fixit Ltd to repair the system. They agreed to complete the necessary work within one week.

Owing to supply problems, the work was not completed within the week and Fixit offered to install a temporary system which would enable half-day working at the factory. Millicent rejected this offer. In the event, the repair work took two months and as a result Millicent lost a highly remunerative contract to supply knitwear to the armed forces. Millicent is now claiming a total of £8,000 by way of lost profits.

Advise Fixit Ltd as to their liability in damages.

Further, consider the position if the contract between Millicent and Fixit referred to above had contained the following provision: "If the repair work is not completed within one week, Fixit shall pay Millicent, by way of agreed damages, the sum of £5,000 plus £2,000 for every week during which the work is unfinished."

General guidance

In some respects the topic of remedies is one of the most important areas of contract at law. Issues involving remedies can appear in *any* question on the law of contract as a subsidiary issue. We saw an example of this in Chapter 2, where a sample question on offer and acceptance raised an issue relating to damages. However, where questions concentrate on remedies, there are two main areas upon which questions could be based.

The first is the remedy of damages for breach of contract. The award of damages in contract raises two main issues: remoteness of damage, i.e. for what types of loss is the defendant to be liable; and measure of damages, i.e. how is the court to quantify the claimant's loss. Measure of damages raises further matters: contributory negligence, mitigation and damages for mental distress. You can expect a problem question to address most, if not all, of these issues. There are also the special rules relating to penalties and liquidated damages; this could merit a question all of its own or be mixed in with other issues as in the sample question above.

The second area that a question on remedies might relate to is equitable remedies. The main equitable remedies are specific performance and injunction which are available, not as of right, but at the discretion of the court. Questions are likely to focus on the point that these remedies will only be granted where it is equitable to do so, and may be refused on the grounds of hardship. As with all equitable remedies, they may be denied where the claimant has acted unconscionably, in accordance with the maxim, "He who comes to equity must come with clean hands".

Model answer

Fixit are in breach of contract and the first issue to be considered is the extent of their liability. Millicent is claiming a total of £8,000 by way of lost profits and it may be that some of that loss is too remote.

The test of remoteness for damages in breach of contract was originally laid down in *Hadley v Baxendale*, 1854 and refined in subsequent cases, notably *The Heron II*, HL, 1969. The position is that the claimant may recover for such loss as arises naturally out of the breach, i.e. according to the usual course of things as the probable result of the breach, or, in the case of special or unusual loss, if the loss could reasonably be supposed to have been within the contemplation of the parties, at the time of the contract, as the probable result of the breach.

REMEDIES

Applying these principles to the facts in question, it is clear that Fixit must have envisaged loss of normal business profits, but whether they should be liable for the loss of the "highly remunerative" contract may depend on the state of their knowledge at the time of the contract. It is possible that this loss is too remote. In *Victoria Laundry (Windsor) Ltd v Newman Industries Ltd*, CA, 1949, the defendants agreed to sell the claimants a boiler. The defendants knew it was required for the claimants' immediate use in their business of launderers and dyers. Delivery was five months late in breach of contract by the defendants. The plaintiffs claimed loss of profits; (i) £16 per week representing the loss of "normal" new business they would have taken on; and (ii) £262 per week which they could have earned under lucrative dyeing contracts with the Ministry of Supply. The Court of Appeal held that the defendants' knowledge was such as to render them liable for (i), but not (ii) about which they knew nothing.

Further, there is a duty on the claimant to mitigate his loss, i.e. he cannot recover in respect of loss that could reasonably have been avoided; *British Westinghouse Electric Co v Underground Electric Railway Co*, HL, 1912. Here, Fixit have offered to install a temporary heating system and Millicent has rejected the offer and so the question may turn on whether this refusal was reasonable in the circumstances. The burden of proving the failure to mitigate will lie on Fixit.

If the contract had contained the provision referred to in the last paragraph of the question, the court would have to consider the nature of the provision. If the provision can be regarded as a genuine pre-estimate of the loss (a liquidated or agreed damages clause), the claimant will be able to recover the sum stipulated without proof of loss. Alternatively, if it is held to be in the nature of a threat to compel the other party to perform (a penalty), the provision will be invalid and the claimant may recover only for the loss he has actually suffered.

Guidelines for distinguishing between liquidated damages and penalty were laid down by the House of Lords in *Dunlop Pneumatic Tyre Co Ltd v New Garage and Motor Co Ltd*, HL, 1915, some of which may be relevant here. Thus, the fact that the provision is referred to as "agreed damages" will not prevent it being a penalty if that is its true nature. In particular, if the sum is extravagant and unconscionable in comparison with the greatest loss which could conceivably follow the breach, the sum may be regarded as a penalty.

In the question, Millicent's claim for damages (including items that may be too remote) amounts to £8,000, whereas under the provision in the contract, after eight weeks' delay, some £19,000 would be payable. In view of this it is at least arguable that the provision is in the nature of a penalty and not recoverable. Millicent would be entitled to recover for her actual loss.

Handy Hints and Useful Websites

HANDY HINTS

Once you have studied the preceding chapters, you might like to test your knowledge and understanding by pitting your wits against the examination checklist of questions given below. If your knowledge is hazy and you need to jog your memory, refer back to the appropriate point in the relevant chapter. Use this method as part of your revision.

It should also be helpful, when revising, to review once more the sample questions and answers given at the end of each chapter from Chapter 2 onwards. You will have seen that, in addition to either a Model answer or an Answer plan, there is General guidance on examination questions on the particular topic and how to approach them.

In addition to committing the law to memory, thinking about how you will answer questions on a particular topic is an important part of your preparation for the examination. Obviously, in an unseen examination you will not know in advance the particular questions and topics that will come up in the examination. But by carefully reviewing the questions your tutors have set you in seminars and coursework, you should learn *something* about *the type* of questions that are likely to face you in the examination. Use that knowledge wisely in your revision.

EXAMINATION REVISION CHECKLIST

CHAPTER 1

(1)   What do you understand by the concept of "freedom of contract"?

CHAPTER 2

(2)   When will the parties, viewed objectively, have reached agreement? What is the distinction between an offer and an invitation to treat?

(3)   When will the offer have been unequivocally accepted? What is a counter-offer? What is required in order successfully to revoke an offer?

(4)   When does the postal rule apply?

. . . .

CHAPTER 3

(5)   In what particular types of agreement does the law presume that there is no intention to create legal relations? How is the presumption to be rebutted?

. . . .

CHAPTER 4

(6)   What is meant by "consideration"? When is the consideration "past"? What is the position regarding the performance of, or the promise to perform;
  (a) an existing public duty; or
  (b) an existing contractual duty; or
  (c) an existing contractual duty owed to a third party.

(7)   Under what circumstances will the part-payment of a debt furnish consideration?

(8)   Explain what is meant by "promissory estoppel"? What are the requirements which must be satisfied before the doctrine comes into play?

. . . .

CHAPTER 5

(9)   Explain which contracts are enforceable against minors.

(10) What is meant by the requirement that a contract should be "evidenced in writing"? To which type of contract does it apply?

. . . .

CHAPTER 6

(11) What are the guidelines for distinguishing between representations and terms?

(12) Explain and distinguish between conditions, warranties and innominate terms.

(13) In what three ways will terms be implied into a contract?

(14) In a contract governed by the Sale of Goods Act 1979, what terms will be implied?

CHAPTER 7

(15) In what ways may exclusion clauses be incorporated into the contract?

(16) What is meant by saying that exclusion clauses will be construed contra proferentem?

(17) How does the Unfair Contract Terms Act 1977 deal with the attempt to exclude the following types of liability?

    (a) sale of goods and hire purchase (s.6);

    (b) supply of goods and services (s.7);

    (c) negligence liability (s.2);

    (d) liability for breach of contract (s.3).

(18) Where the reasonableness test in s.11 of the 1977 Act applies, what factors are relevant?

(19) Explain how the law deals with unfair terms in consumer contracts.

CHAPTER 8

(20) What is the definition of actionable misrepresentation?

(21) What is the rule about silence in relation to misrepresentation and what are the exceptions to it?

(22) Distinguish between fraudulent, negligent and innocent misrepresentation and the consequences of each. What remedies are available at common law; in equity; and under the Misrepresentation Act 1967?

(23) When will the right to rescind a contract for misrepresentation be lost?

CHAPTER 9

(24) Explain the circumstances in which the remedy of *non est factum* will be available?

(25) What is the distinction between a common, mutual and unilateral mistake? When will such mistakes be operative?

(26) How is a common mistake as to quality dealt with at common law?

(27) When will a unilateral mistake as to identity be operative?

CHAPTER 10

(28) Distinguish between duress and undue influence.

(29) What is the distinction between actual and presumed undue influence?

In what circumstances might a third party to a contract be affected by undue influence?

CHAPTER 11

(30) Explain the categories of contract that are illegal on the ground that they are contrary to public policy

(31) Which contracts fall within the restraint of trade doctrine? What are the two traditional proprietary interests that merit protection?

(32) In relation to the validity of covenants in restraint of trade, explain:
- (a) "flexible" construction; and
- (b) the doctrine of severance.

CHAPTER 12

(33) How did the Contracts (Rights of Third Parties) Act 1999 modify the law of privity?

(34) What are the established exceptions to the rule of privity?

CHAPTER 13

(35) What are the four ways in which a contract may be discharged?

(36) What is the test for determining whether a contract has been frustrated?

(37) Give examples of impossibility, illegality or a radical change in the circumstances leading to frustration.

(38) What are the exceptions to the rule about precise performance?

CHAPTER 14

(39) Under the rules of remoteness of damage in contract, explain the different treatment of;
- (a) normal loss; and
- (b) special, abnormal or unusual loss.

(40) When will the claimant be under a duty to mitigate the loss in a claim for damages?

(41) What is the difference between "penalty" and "liquidated damages". What guidelines have been laid down in order to distinguish between them?

(42) What are the limitations, in contract cases, upon the grant of injunctions and orders of specific performance?

USEFUL WEBSITES

www.lawcom.gov.uk—the site contains reports of the Law Commission on proposals to reform the law.

www.opsi.gov.uk—the website of the Office of Public Sector Information; contains primary and delegated legislation on contract and other legal subjects, including the Unfair Contract Terms Act 1977.

www.privy-council.org.uk—the site contains law reports of decisions of the Judicial Committee of the Privy Council.

www.supremecourt.gov.uk—the site contains law reports of judgments of the Supreme Court.

Index

This index has been prepared using Sweet and Maxwell's Legal Taxonomy. Main index entries conform to keywords provided by the Legal Taxonomy except where references to specific documents or non-standard terms (denoted by quotation marks) have been included. These keywords provide a means of identifying similar concepts in other Sweet and Maxwell publications and on-line services to which keywords from the Legal Taxonomy have been applied. Readers may find some differences between terms used in the text and those which appear in the index.